MW01632246

The Benevon Model for Sustainable Funding

A Step-by-Step Guide to Getting it Right

Terry Axelrod

The Benevon Model for Sustainable Funding:
A Step-by-Step Guide to Getting it Right

Terry Axelrod

Benevon (formerly Raising More Money) Publications, Seattle, Washington

The following trademarks appear throughout this book:

Benevon®, Point of Entry®, Next Step®, Free Feel-Good Cultivation Event™, Cultivation Superhighway™, Free One-Hour Ask Event™, Essential Story™, Visionary Leader™, Emotional Hook™, Multiple-Year Giving Society™, Units of Service™, Five-Step Follow-Up Call™.

For information, please contact:
Benevon Publications, 4528 8th Avenue NE, Suite 1A, Seattle, WA 98105

First edition published in 2012.

ISBN: 978-0-615-65232-0

The Library of Congress Cataloging-in-Publication Data
is available from the publisher.

For information, please contact:
Benevon Publications
4528 8th Avenue NE, Suite 1A, Seattle, WA 98105
888-322-9357

TABLE OF CONTENTS

ACKNOWLEDGEMENTS

Over the past 16 years, since Benevon began, our staff has been deeply committed to only one thing: developing and refining a model for building sustainable funding from individual donors.

Like mad scientists working feverishly in the laboratory, we have systematically analyzed the real-world application of the Benevon Model for Sustainable Funding with each of the more than 4,000 nonprofit teams that we have trained, many of whom have been with us five years or longer. Each two-day workshop or coaching call has provided the rich field data we have needed to refine and synthesize this process to its simplest principles, which can be adopted by any group willing to do the work to get it right.

For that reason, I am most grateful to these pioneering teams of dedicated board members, staff, and volunteers who have worked to shift the culture within their organizations to one that fosters the long-term engagement of individual donors. It takes a lot of guts to realize there is life beyond the annual gala or golf tournament, to come into our Benevon 101 Workshop and Coaching Program, and to do the real work needed to follow our rigorous coaching, year after year, particularly when it runs counter to conventional wisdom.

Thanks to our remarkable coaches and instructors for standing for a new reality of sustainable funding and abundance for nonprofits, and for their finely tuned radar that has allowed us to significantly improve the model over time: to Sharon Ervine, Benevon curriculum director and my exceptional partner in creating and deepening our curriculum; to Laura Fixler, our instructor and coach extraordinaire; and to Marcy McNeal, powerful coach and leader.

Thanks to Suzanne Shoemaker, Benevon vice president, for "walking the talk." Thank you for seeing that the Point of Entry Event is the magic of the Benevon Model and for sharing with me your vision that, someday, every nonprofit would be hosting simple Point of Entry Events as a way to educate and inspire individuals in their communities about their work.

Thanks to our laser-sharp, warm-hearted staff team at Benevon for the vital role you have played in creating this enduring body of work. I know that each of you has chosen to work at Benevon because of the impact our work is having every day.

Thanks to our outstanding editorial and publications team for their invaluable expertise, particularly Melissa Lound, my steadfast in-house editor, and to Ann Overton, Miriam Walsh Lisco, Leslie Eliel, and Paulette Eickman, who each played a major role in helping me to clarify the message and make this book a reality. As so many have told me, "It's one thing to be able to teach it and another thing altogether to be able to write it as a book."

And finally, a forever thank-you to my husband Alan, whose constant support and encouragement have fueled Benevon since the very first day.

INTRODUCTION

I started Benevon with only one distinct intention: to give nonprofits a step-by-step process for attaining sustainable funding from individual donors.

Sixteen years later the Benevon staff and I have learned so much, and Benevon has earned a reputation for its success in working with all types and sizes of nonprofit organizations.

In fact, so many people have heard of or been exposed to some part of the Benevon Model, it comes as no surprise that some would want to fit those pieces into their existing fundraising efforts.

Yet the Benevon Model for Sustainable Funding is a finely-tuned system of complex and interdependent processes, and to be successful, it must be implemented in its entirety, following the specific processes and formulas I will describe in this book.

This book synthesizes the most critical learnings of the Benevon Model and makes them available for first-time implementers. It is designed for small to mid-sized nonprofits who want to get started on their own and who want to do it right. While this will not take the place of working with Benevon directly, those who carefully follow the tried and tested directions in this book will not waste their time and will avoid the biggest mistakes of self-implementation.

Many parts of the Benevon Model are counterintuitive; that is, they seem exactly the opposite of what you might think works best. Why, for example, begin your Ask Event at the scheduled time if not everyone has taken their seats? Shouldn't you wait another 10 minutes to begin, being flexible with these people whom you are about to ask for support? The answer is no. You may think that doesn't make any sense, but 16 years of experience with more than a million guests at Ask Events has taught us that what works best is to begin at the scheduled time.

This book is based on the hard-won wisdom that only comes from painstaking and extensive work in the field. If you are willing to take on and follow the rules distilled from what we have learned, you will be rewarded with a breakthrough in sustainable funding for your organization.

Terry Axelrod

THE BENEVON TRACK RECORD

Nonprofit organizations enrolled in the year-long Benevon 101 Workshop and Coaching Program since we began in 1996.	*4,000 teams from organizations of every size and type*
Each organization has a team of seven board members, staff, and volunteers who attend the Benevon 101 Workshop and Coaching Program, where we customize the Benevon Model for their organization and then coach them for a year to take the lead in implementing it successfully.	*28,000 trained individuals*
Each team puts on 20 or more Point of Entry Events for 10 to 15 guests each year.	*800,000 Point of Entry guests*
Each group puts on an annual Ask Event for approximately 250 people.	*More than 1,000,000 Ask Event guests*

CHAPTER 1

THE POWER OF GETTING IT RIGHT

Even with the best of intentions and a lot of hard work, many nonprofit organizations find themselves stuck with a tired old-reality fundraising system that leaves them powerless to do much more than get by from year to year.

The Old Reality: Jumping on the Annual Fundraising Treadmill

Fundraising methods for nonprofits have not changed much in the last 50 years: write a grant proposal, put on a party, have board members write letters or call their friends for money. All of this worked well enough, one year at a time.

Raising $50,000 to $100,000 at a gala, auction, or golf tournament was plenty to get the job done for the coming year. Board members dutifully filled tables, sold tickets, and solicited the same friends who had solicited them earlier in the year for their favorite cause. They bucked up and did that dreaded fundraising thing, raising enough money to keep the doors open for another year.

It was a zero-sum game. The same big donors in the community giving roughly the same amount of money they gave the year before. But if you were to ask those donors to describe their deeper, long-term connection to the organization to which they wrote their check, most would tell you

Year-to-year "treadmill" fundraising was and is hard work. It has burnout written all over it.

they barely remembered the name of the charity, or they would say, "I just did it because my friend asked me to."

From the nonprofit's point of view, the story was even more tiresome. Smart, eager development professionals jumped onto an already fast-moving treadmill of fundraising, never able to stop and challenge the fundamental assumptions. They inherited a juggling act of many disparate pieces and, with no alternative method to recommend, they fell in step with the status quo—writing grants, producing the next big event, urging board members to make calls and write letters.

Year-to-year "treadmill" fundraising was and is hard work. It has burnout written all over it. Is it any wonder that the average tenure of a development director is under two years? Or that the dream job of almost every development director is to work at a big university or private foundation?

The long-term impact of this approach on each organization is especially debilitating. Smart boards hire smart executive directors, who hire smart development directors, who turn over every two years. They never have the time to build long-term, sustainable relationships with donors, to engage them in the organization's real work, or to give them the opportunity to make a lasting contribution to a mission they believe in.

The New Reality: Building a System of Sustainable Funding

Like the old system of fundraising, the new system of sustainable funding relies heavily on relationships. In the old reality, board members and volunteers prevailed on friends to buy tickets, sponsor tables at special events, write checks, or make grants. But eventually they moved on to the board of another nonprofit organization, taking their relationships with them.

"To think that someone of Martin's caliber fell in love with the school in his own right and could carry on the leadership of our board—that is remarkable!"

What if those same precious relationships could be used differently? Rather than rushing to the "Ask," using the old strong-arm solicitation approach of the past, what if your board members and volunteers used that same trusted relationship to invite their friends and colleagues to your organization's engaging and compelling one-hour Point of Entry Events and let the guests decide for themselves if your work mattered enough to them to get involved?

That is precisely what happened during the two years I worked as the first development director at an urban academy in Seattle, where I began to develop the Benevon Model.

Our board members all truly loved the school and had joined the board because they really cared. They had each already spent time at the school and had listened to and responded to the powerful vision of the school's founders.

So once we created and began to hold our introductory tours, now called Point of Entry Events, on a regular basis, the board members happily invited friends to attend, often joining them for the tour and then taking their friends to breakfast or lunch afterwards. Eventually, the board members realized they could trust me to take good care of their friends, so they invited them to the Point of Entry Events without joining the tours themselves.

I remember the first time one of their guests, Martin, fell in love with the school. As he was leaving his first Point of Entry Event, Martin turned and said to me, "This was amazing! How do I get on the board here?" When I called our board chair, John, to tell him what his friend had said, he was stunned. "He actually said that? Do you know how great that makes me feel? To think that someone of Martin's caliber fell in love with the school in his own right and could carry on the leadership of our board—that is remarkable!" Martin, like many others after him, joined the board and provided strong leadership for many years.

Each of our board members was discovering the same thing: it was far more effective to invite their friends and colleagues to a Point of Entry Event…

Compare that outcome to the old approach. John could have taken Martin out for lunch and asked him to write a check to this great inner-city school. Martin would have obliged dutifully. End of story. Or perhaps John and his wife could have invited Martin and his wife to join them at an annual gala or golf tournament, where there would be even less of a connection with the school's mission.

Instead, we cultivated the relationship with Martin after the Point of Entry Event. I made a Five-Step Follow-Up Call three days later and asked him what he thought of the school and the tour. How else might he like to become involved? Was there anyone he might like to invite to attend a tour?

The result was that Martin became what we now call an Ambassador, inviting first his family and then his business associates to tour the school. As we followed up with his friends and family, many of them got involved with the school, and Martin became more involved as well. He was a Table Captain at our first Free One-Hour Ask Event about nine months later; seven of his nine guests had already attended Point of Entry Events. Three of them joined our Multiple-Year Giving Society, pledging $1,000 a year for each of the next five years. One other guest, in addition to Martin himself, pledged $5,000 a year for five years.

That one referral—based strictly on John's relationship with Martin—led to pledges totaling $65,000. And the ripple effect was just beginning. Martin sat on the board of a private foundation, ran a company, and had many other relationships with people he was excited to introduce to the school.

Each of our board members was discovering the same thing: it was far more effective to invite their friends and colleagues to a Point of Entry Event, to merely make the introduction and leave it to their guest to choose to become involved or not, than it was to ask them to write a check to the school.

The people who came to the Ask Event were the same people who had already attended the Points of Entry and had specifically expressed interest in staying involved with the organization.

Because they had attended the Point of Entry Events many times themselves, board members knew their friends would be inspired and educated about the school in that hour, whether or not they ever chose to become involved. They also knew that after the Follow-Up Call I would "bless and release" those guests who did not want to become involved, so there would be no awkwardness the next time they saw their friend. At that point, it would be the organization's job to develop an ongoing relationship between the donor and the school, and ultimately for asking for money if that was appropriate.

The first year, we did that asking at the Ask Event. The people who came to the Ask Event were the same people who had already attended the Points of Entry and had specifically expressed interest in staying involved with the organization. They knew they were going to be asked for money. In fact, many wondered why no one had asked them sooner.

Those relationships between board members, volunteers, staff, and their friends and colleagues had been used to build new relationships between potential donors and the organization itself. Now it would be up to the staff to develop and manage those relationships skillfully, over time, involving volunteers as appropriate, to cultivate each major donor and grow a strong major-gifts program.

Now It Is Your Turn: Getting It Right

Perhaps you have never heard of the Benevon Model and have been hired as the new development director for a nonprofit organization that believes they have been implementing the Benevon Model correctly, yet they are only doing one piece of it: the Free One-Hour Ask Event. Your assignment is to put on a successful Ask Event three months from now.

Or perhaps you are already familiar with the Benevon Model and have been hired by an organization that is not

Be forewarned: You are embarking on a process that is fundamentally different from the way fundraising has always been done.

using this model at all. Their annual gala is coming up in the spring, the holiday mailing needs to go out next, and four grant deadlines are rapidly approaching. Your marching orders from the executive director are, "Please save the day and do it all." You care deeply about the work of this organization and, even though you are planning to work here for only a year or two, you want to use that time to free them of the old-reality fundraising treadmill and build a lasting legacy of sustainable funding. Your goal is to leave them with the Benevon Model firmly in place.

You want to do it right. You are one person with the best of intentions.

Be forewarned: you are embarking on a process that is fundamentally different from the way fundraising has always been done. And like a bold explorer venturing out to discover new lands, there is much unknown territory ahead.

Many other smart, good people before you have tried this. Here is what those who have been successful would tell you:

1. *Assemble a great team.* Do not try this alone. You need a team. Take the time at the beginning to get others on board with the model and form a working team of seven to eight board members, staff, and volunteers. Have them all watch the Benevon video or read this book so they understand the larger implications of what they will be setting out to accomplish. Ask them to make a one-year commitment to work with you to implement the entire model successfully.

   Make sure they know this is not just about putting on an Ask Event. In fact, the Benevon Model is not about events; it is a systematic process for engaging and developing relationships with individual donors who will want to support your organization for the long term.

Do not let the Benevon Model or the process of implementing it become staff-driven.

2. *Insist on full-team participation.* Do not let the Benevon Model or the process of implementing it become staff-driven. Yes, the executive director and development staff need to be fully committed to this approach, but without equal involvement from board members and volunteers, it will never work, so take the time to educate them and get them on board. If you find that the staff is doing all of the inviting of guests to Point of Entry Events, you are on the wrong track.

3. *Preserve the integrity of the Benevon Model.* Make sure all your team members understand the complete Benevon Model and agree to follow it exactly as it is designed *without getting creative.* At first, your team may not understand the significance of never deviating from or improvising on the Benevon Model. Over the first year, especially, there will be innumerable temptations to modify and tweak the model, even if ever so slightly, yet in ways that can derail your entire implementation.

   Granted, we all like to be creative, we all have good ideas, and we certainly are always on the lookout for shortcuts. But the Benevon Model is a whole and complete system, as precise as the system a professional organization would use for managing accounting or human resources. No matter how well-intentioned you and your team members are, you cannot know the subtleties and many counterintuitive aspects of the Benevon Model. We have tested and refined every aspect and detail of the model with more than 4,000 nonprofit teams over more than 16 years.

You must allow for 9 to 12 months of successful Point of Entry Events before your first Ask Event.

4. *Prepare thoroughly for the Ask.* Do not rush into the Ask Event, or into one-on-one Asks for Leadership or Challenge Gifts. You must allow for 9 to 12 months of successful Point of Entry Events before your first Ask Event.

5. *Implement every formula.* Finally, follow all the formulas we have worked out for you in the Benevon Model:
   - Two Point of Entry Events per month with 10 to 15 people in attendance.
   - 100% of Ask Event Table Captains have served as successful Ambassadors in the prior 12 months, having at least 10 guests attend Points of Entry.
   - At least 40% of Ask Event guests have attended a Point of Entry Event in the prior 12 months.
   - 10% of Ask Event guests join the Multiple-Year Giving Society newly each year.
   - Multiple-Year Giving Society: the minimum gift level to join is $1,000 a year for five-year pledge; levels are either: $1,000, $5,000, and $10,000 or $1,000, $10,000, and $25,000, all for five years.
   - Expect 40% to 50% of Ask Event guests to make a gift of any amount. Expect remaining guests to give nothing.
   - Have a Challenge or Leadership Gift of at least $5,000 to announce at the first Ask Event.
   - Benevon's definition of a successful Ask Event: take your final actual number of Ask Event guests, divide by two, and multiply by $1,000 to get your expected total (e.g., an Ask Event with 200 people should raise a minimum of $100,000 in cash and pledges).

Implementing the Benevon Model takes time, money, hard work, and a commitment to getting it right.

If you and your team are not seriously committed to following these five basic rules and implementing the Benevon Model according to the 12 steps laid out in this book, I strongly recommend that you stop reading now.

Implementing the Benevon Model takes time, money, hard work, and a commitment to getting it right. Without a firm, long-term commitment—especially when the going gets tough—your board and donors will confuse this model with the fundraising fad of the day and change courses when they hit the first speed bump.

If you choose to keep reading, however, you will have in your hands a step-by-step guide to getting it right the first time and building a lasting legacy for your organization.

CHAPTER 2

WHAT IT WILL TAKE TO CREATE A LASTING LEGACY OF SUSTAINABLE FUNDING

What if you could leave the legacy of an ongoing, systematic process, one that would engage and develop relationships with individual donors passionate about seeing the work and mission of your organization fulfilled in the world? The Benevon Model is designed to do just that.

Imagine coming back to your favorite nonprofit organization 20 years from now. Let's assume that no one remembers you, nor do you recognize anyone who is currently involved there. Everyone looks very young—and happy! As you walk around, you notice that great work is getting done. Many new programs have emerged—the kinds of programs you and your colleagues dreamed about 20 years ago. More clients are being served, with more effective services, by well-paid, dedicated staff. Those old, run-down offices are all spiffed-up and modernized.

You can't help but feel the energy around the place. Confidence and optimism are the order of the day. People know that they are winning the game—whether it is preventing child abuse, expanding the arts, or protecting the environment.

One thing is distinctly missing from back in your era: no one seems to be suffering about funding. There appears to be plenty of money to allow staff to focus on doing the best work possible and producing the very best outcomes.

This future is possible for your favorite nonprofit organization.

You can't help but ask someone, "What happened? Back in my day, we were always hampered by the lack of funds. It seems like no one here is worried about the money anymore."

"Money?" they reply, quizzically. "Oh, we handled that several years ago. We have a steady source of unrestricted funds we can use for whatever we know needs to happen next. Our job is to focus now on fulfilling the mission of the organization. We have the luxury of never worrying about the money."

Even more stunned, you ask again, "What happened?"

"I don't really know, firsthand," replies the young staff member. "But from what I've heard, 10 or 15 years ago there was a group of people who were so dedicated to our mission that they committed to raise an endowment fund large enough that the earnings or interest from that endowment would fund our operating gap every year. The way the story goes, that process engaged so many individuals in what our work is really all about that, almost overnight, everyone knew about us, and we had all kinds of new passionate supporters from every part of the community. Up until then, we had been called the best-kept secret in town."

"That is so great to hear," you reply, incredulously.

"Yep," smiles the young staff member. "I never knew any of those people, but we can't thank them enough for having the vision and commitment to figure out the funding. If you'll excuse me now, I've got to get back to work."

This future is possible for your favorite nonprofit organization. Here is what a financially self-sustaining nonprofit organization looks like:

- It has a self-generating group of enthusiastic individual donors who know your work and mission and *who consider it consistent with their own values and mission in life*. They regard their contributions to your organization as a bold step toward the fulfillment of their own purpose.

What began as a mere fundraising program has become an ongoing operating system for engaging and developing relationships with individuals who will sustain your work and, in turn, engage others to do the same.

- These loyal donors understand your work and freely choose to pledge their ongoing financial support by making unrestricted gifts for your operational needs and some of these donors also give for capital projects and an endowment fund. Rather than developing separate categories of donors to give to operations, capital, and endowment, this ever-increasing, single pool of loyal donors is what you draw upon to support all of these needs. These individual donors and supporters also advocate on behalf of your group at the legislature or invest in the continuing education of your staff. They are there to help fund a one-time special need for a family or community. They care *that* much!

- Your donors engage others naturally by consistently talking about their favorite nonprofit organization with their friends and colleagues. They do this not because they have to sell tickets or raise dollars before the end of the year, but because they are genuinely excited about the organization's work, and they want to tell others about it.

- As time goes on, a ripple effect takes hold. Instead of board members needing to ask their friends for money, people who have gotten to know your organization over time begin to come to you and ask how they can join your board or help you in other ways. What began as a mere fundraising program has become an ongoing operating system for engaging and developing relationships with individuals who will sustain your work and, in turn, engage others to do the same.

No longer the "best-kept secret in town," your organization is well on the way to fulfilling its mission with a strong cadre of supporters who are delighted to be involved.

- Far beyond being your bread and butter, these loyal and passionate supporters are your oxygen, breathing life and vitality into your nonprofit organization, regularly refreshing your board, your volunteers, your staff, and keeping your organization connected to the current needs of the community. No longer the "best-kept secret in town," your organization is well on the way to fulfilling its mission with a strong cadre of supporters who are delighted to be involved.

Confronting the Idea that It Can't Be Done

Often when an organization begins a major initiative, they count on the enthusiasm for new beginnings to carry them over the barriers they are sure to encounter. One of the unique and powerful aspects of the Benevon Model is that it takes on and addresses those barriers as integral parts of implementing a successful, overall system of sustainable funding.

There are seven conversations that typically arise as barriers to implementing the Benevon Model. It will help if you can recognize those that apply to your organization so you can better prepare yourself and your team to deal with them.

Barrier 1: We don't see how an organization like ours could ever have a "fundraising" board.

- Our mission isn't as appealing as other groups, such as those organizations dealing with the arts, the environment, or children's groups.
- We are in a small or low-income community. Our board members are community members, family members of the constituents we serve, or professionals in our field. They are not the big donors in our town.

"Our work is highly confidential. We cannot ethically reveal the stories of the people we serve."

- Our board has never been asked to do anything like this before.

Barrier 2: We don't see how a group like ours could ever have programs that are fully funded.

- Our work is unique and very few people really understand it well enough. [This is often heard about policy work, advocacy work, research, international relief, or community development work.]
- Even when people do understand our work, they see it as a bottomless pit. How would we ever quantify the financial gap we need to fill? It's a moving target.
- "Fully funded" would send the wrong message to the community. People would think our funding is handled and they would stop giving to us.

Barrier 3: It is not possible for an organization like ours to be known in the community for all the great work we really do.

- Our work is highly confidential. We cannot ethically reveal the stories of the people we serve.
- We have so many complex programs scattered across the state or region or world. How can we possibly explain all of this to outsiders?
- We don't have the staff time available to dedicate to spreading the word. This isn't enough of a priority.
- If we did get the word out, people would be clamoring at our doors wanting to give us advice and thinking they know better how to do our work.

Barrier 4: It is not possible for an organization like ours to effectively communicate the results we produce and the real impact we have on people's lives.

- Our work has long-term impact, we are changing social systems, and we are breaking down generations of prejudice. None of these results show up overnight.

"People will think that changing our approach or trying something new means we don't know what we're doing."

- To say we changed the life of one prisoner or advocated on behalf of one person with a disability doesn't sound like a lot. It doesn't sound nearly as impressive as a food bank that serves thousands of people.
- Our issue isn't attractive—people don't care that we produce great results with homeless men or substance abusers.

Barrier 5: It is not possible for an organization like ours to talk openly with donors about the trends we see in our field.

- People barely understand what we do anyway. How will they be able to understand how much our field is changing?
- The trends are getting worse. People think our issue is hopeless and inevitable.
- People don't want to hear about our issue—it's scary.
- If people knew the trends and wanted to help us anyway, it would mean more work for us, managing more volunteers who have opinions and make requests that take time to answer.
- The trends show our issue is getting better, therefore people won't feel an urgency to support us.

Barrier 6: It is not possible for an organization like ours to experiment with a new fundraising program like the Benevon Model even if we feel it could be more effective than what we are currently doing.

- People will think that changing our approach or trying something new means we don't know what we're doing.
- Our funders will stop supporting us if we don't keep doing what we've already proven can work.
- Our donors will be disappointed if we stop having their favorite fundraising event—the auction, the gala, or the golf tournament.

This assumption of scarcity infects our thinking about everything—money, time, resources, volunteers, even caring.

Barrier 7: It is not possible for an organization like ours to be regarded as an organization worthy of long-term financial support from individual donors.

- We are not a major university or hospital with a long history in our community.
- We are too new and unknown for people to pledge long-term support.
- Our mission only impacts a small constituency within the community, so why would new donors be interested in our mission?
- Donors already have their favorite charities picked out.
- We have had recent leadership changes or unfavorable publicity.

Over the past 16 years, working with more than 4,000 nonprofit teams, the Benevon staff has heard and dealt with every possible barrier to change. We take these barriers seriously—we use them to refine and perfect a fundraising model that is sustainable and successful precisely because it includes and addresses those barriers effectively.

All you have to do is follow the step-by-step process to implementation—a process that begins with permanently shifting your thinking.

Moving from Resignation and Scarcity to Possibility and Abundance

Underneath these barriers to change is one big assumption —that in the nonprofit world there will never be enough. This assumption of scarcity infects our thinking about everything—money, time, resources, volunteers, even caring.

Let's use a foster care organization to illustrate how the assumption of scarcity shapes what we see as possible. Beyond concerns about money, the organization may feel there is

And while there may be something appealing—even motivating—about thinking of your organization as an underdog…

not enough public awareness of the number of children in the foster care system, the average number of foster homes a foster child lives in, the percentage of domestic abuse cases that happens in foster homes, or the length of time it takes for each court case or placement. They may say there are not enough legislators aware of the long-term societal impact of having children live their entire childhood years in foster care, not enough people doing anything about the number of children who leave foster care at age 18 with no plan or support for the future. They may feel there are not enough community leaders willing to join their board, to advocate on behalf of foster children, or to adopt foster children. And certainly there are not enough trained staff members to deal with the problem.

The organization thinks of itself as the underdog. They are doing their best with limited resources to impact the foster care system. They cannot reach all the children in need, but each child they do save is better than saving none. And while there may be something appealing—even motivating—about thinking of your organization as an underdog, it can also reinforce a context or worldview of scarcity that assures a long, hard life on the fundraising treadmill.

No one who works in the nonprofit world should have any trouble translating this example into the reality of their own organization. This is business as usual. It is just "the way it is."

The assumption of scarcity, and the feelings of powerlessness to change the way it is, inevitably lead to resignation. We resign ourselves to what we have come to know as the limitations of the system. And more significantly, we resign ourselves to thinking we cannot make the difference we so much want to make.

In order to implement the Benevon Model successfully and scale it to full sustainable funding within your organization, you will need to confront this underlying assumption

I encourage you to have these deeper conversations with yourself and with your staff and volunteer leadership before you embark on implementing the Benevon Model.

of scarcity and the resignation that keeps it in place. That is easier said than done.

Like the poor, urban school in Seattle where the Benevon Model was developed, your organization will need to see itself as being worthy of big support, big money, and big resources. You will need to be willing to shift the context of your organization from one of scarcity, suffering, and survival to a context of possibility and even abundance.

The Challenge

If you are looking to leave a legacy of sustainable funding for your favorite nonprofit, if you are thinking you might be ready to get beyond the year-to-year fundraising treadmill once and for all, the first place to look may be your own limiting thoughts.

- Is your nonprofit organization ready to shift its thinking from scarcity to abundance?
- Are you willing to let go of being resigned about the way it is, to give up all of those things you are sure your organization could never do or have?
- Are you willing to open up the organization to input from the broader community? Do you really want to be *that* transparent and inclusive?

I encourage you to have these deeper conversations with yourself and with your staff and volunteer leadership before you embark on implementing the Benevon Model.

Even after you are certain everyone is ready to move forward, you should expect each newcomer to the process to arrive armed with their own unconscious scarcity thinking. Having them understand what you are truly trying to accomplish will strengthen your own resolve and ultimately attract new believers to your team.

To deal with these challenges, you and your team need to be able to readily tap into your genuine passion for the mission of your organization.

Passion: Your Most Valuable and Renewable Resource

Scarcity and resignation, thinking it can't be done—these are the recurring challenges for anyone committed to big results. To deal with these challenges, you and your team need to be able to readily tap into your genuine passion for the mission of your organization. And there is definitely no scarcity of passion in the nonprofit world if you know where to look for it.

Almost everyone is originally attracted to a cause or organization because its work is something they feel passionate about. Whether that cause is families, foster care, substance abuse, mental illness, international relief, physical or intellectual disabilities, advocacy, faith, the environment, arts, education, healthcare, animal welfare, housing, or public policy, what attracts each person is almost always a prior personal experience. Perhaps they have a family member with that particular disability or a close friend who experienced discrimination due to a mental illness. Perhaps they developed a love of the outdoors as a child, or their passion for science dates back to the first time they looked through a microscope in elementary school science class.

But passion can become buried or lost over time. When that happens, how do you get it back?

The Passion Retread Exercise

We do a small group exercise at our workshops that we call the Passion Retread exercise. Working in the nonprofit sector, the tread on the passion tire sometimes wears thin. So we ask each person in the small group to answer these two simple questions:

- Why do you work or volunteer at this particular organization?

It will bond you as a team and sustain you as you move forward.

- What is it about their unique work or mission that inspires you and keeps you engaged?

While some volunteers will say that they want to give back to the community, when we ask them to take a deeper look, many tell us they feel called to do the work of the organization. For them it is an avocation. Answering these simple questions truthfully, in a small group of dedicated board members, staff, and volunteers, reconnects people to their own passion, to each other, and to the mission of the organization.

I once asked a group of board members from a chapter of the American Lung Association to answer these questions. One of their long-standing board members immediately offered his response. "I know exactly why I'm here," he said. "When my son, Adam, was eight years old, he died in my arms while having an asthma attack. I vowed in that moment to give my life to doing whatever I could to find a cure for childhood asthma so that no other parent would ever have to experience such a tragic and painful loss."

Before you embark on implementing the Benevon Model for Sustainable Funding, do this exercise with your entire team. Ask each person to look more deeply at their own reasons for being involved with the organization. Then give them the time to share their answer to this question with the rest of the group. It will focus each team member on their unique connection to the mission of the organization and add new tread to their passion. It will bond you as a team and sustain you as you move forward.

This exercise also works well for long-standing board members, volunteers, and staff. Most nonprofit organizations do very little to nurture their passion, yet over time any of us can become so caught up in the routine of everyday work that our initial enthusiasm wanes.

In the end, all who participate in the exercise will have renewed energy and enthusiasm for telling the story of the organization to the community.

One group of hospital development staff I coached was getting ready to launch their biggest annual campaign ever. For several of the staff, it would be their tenth or twelfth annual campaign with this organization. They were hardened to the realities of life during campaign time and already dreading it. So we put aside the agenda for our session and instead went around the room, with each person telling the story of how they had come to work at this organization in the first place. It was incredibly moving. They had never done this exercise before. In the space of an hour, the entire mood altered. One by one, you could see them re-enlist in the campaign, renewed, re-energized, and ready to go.

When you sense that your team or board or volunteers are losing energy and inspiration, stop and do the Passion Retread exercise. It does not need to be overly formal or time consuming. Just have people tell their stories. You will be surprised at how effectively it reconnects everyone to their larger reasons for being part of the organization. In the end, all who participate in the exercise will have renewed energy and enthusiasm for telling the story of the organization to the community. They will be reminded of just how important the work of this organization is and why they want to be a part of it.

You Need a System for Sustainable Funding

It should be clear by now that implementing the Benevon Model requires more than new actions; it requires new thinking. The mentality and ideas of the old reality of fundraising must give way to new ideas—ideas which will challenge what we already know and that often will seem counter to our experience or intuition. Change disrupts our routines, our familiar ways of doing things. We crave the feeling of certainty, of knowing what we are doing—even if it is less than successful.

...your fundraising could become as predictable and reliable as the payroll system or any other sustainable system you have in your organization.

Few of us working in the nonprofit world have thought about fundraising as a system. Instead, we see it from the old-reality view of getting by with smatterings of direct mail, grant writing, and special events. We have survived by thinking on our feet, being constantly creative, and doing whatever was necessary. All of which has left us on an unsatisfying and unsustainable treadmill, vulnerable to trying the next wild idea that comes along.

Yet when you look at any established and well-run organization, you see that it employs a variety of systems designed to weather the ups and downs of its particular environment. Hospitals, for example, which deal with many staff and patients, have payroll systems, accounting systems, and personnel systems that help navigate and mitigate those realities. They also have elaborate patient record systems, procedures for sterilization, meal service, power backups, and more. They have protocols for everything. They don't try out a new approach with each patient who comes through their doors. They stick with the system.

These systems endure when the hospital chief executive retires, the board chair moves on, or the head of a department leaves to take a new job. Clients, patients, and staff don't suffer. In fact, they may not even know there has been such a change. Nurses and lab technicians keep getting their paychecks and their annual reviews. Life does not come to a halt when one key person leaves. And when the next chief executive comes in, that person does not immediately try to modify the systems that are working. They trust the systems that work.

If you had a proven system that everyone on the team agreed to follow step by step, without deviating or getting creative, your fundraising could become as predictable and reliable as the payroll system or any other sustainable system you have in your organization.

The Benevon Model for Sustainable Funding is that system.

CHAPTER 3

THE BENEVON MODEL FOR SUSTAINABLE FUNDING

The Benevon Model is a model for creating sustainable funding for nonprofit organizations. It has been tested and measured with more than 4,000 teams of dedicated board members, staff, and volunteers who have participated in our training and coaching programs for at least one year. Our metrics-based practices and formulas have been honed and refined week by week, group by group. We leave nothing to chance.

What is a model?
Model: a simplified representation of a system or phenomenon, as in the sciences or economics. (www.dictionary.com)

Most nonprofits are familiar with models, especially in the program areas of their work. There are models for child development, models for teaching reading, models for civic engagement, and models for healthcare delivery.

Why do people use models? Because they provide a framework and a structure for what works.

A robust model appears simple yet its structure allows for great complexity. The more you work with it, the more it informs your thinking. The more its complexities meld with your organization's day-to-day life, the more familiar and natural it seems.

This model has been implemented by nonprofit organizations of all types and sizes, from tiny, start-up, grassroots organizations to large universities.

Models are durable. The model your school uses to teach math or science may not change fundamentally over the years. If one math teacher leaves a school midyear, parents do not need to worry that their children will be taught a whole new method of mathematics from the new teacher. A model or system can be followed continuously, regardless of turnover or the preferences of the individuals who implement it.

People welcome models. They welcome tested systems and structures for getting the job done. And certainly, when it comes to building sustainable funding for a nonprofit organization, a time-tested, results-based model—one that is not dependent on the current development director, the trendiest special event, or the strong-arming of friends by board members—is good news to nonprofit leaders.

The Benevon Model for Sustainable Funding appears to be simple: a circular, four-step process that systematically allows organizations to educate, inspire, involve, and cultivate relationships with the people who want to become more involved, then ask them to make significant multiple-year pledges for unrestricted operating funds and, eventually, for capital and endowment gifts. These satisfied, passionate donors, in turn, introduce others.

In its application, the Benevon Model is quite complex. Far from being a cookie-cutter approach, the model must be customized to each nonprofit organization's unique mission, size, structure, and evolutionary stage as an organization.

This model has been implemented by nonprofit organizations of all types and sizes, from tiny, start-up, grassroots organizations to large universities. We have worked with organizations that focus on policy, advocacy, research, international relief, the environment, healthcare, the arts, human services, housing, schools, and faith, as well as with "umbrella" funding groups, national chapter-based organizations, and many more.

This model has been effective in nonprofit organizations with budgets as small as $150,000 up to over $100 million, in communities with a population size as low as 5,000 up to major metropolitan areas like New York City and Los Angeles.

We find the main predictor of success is not the size of the community or the size of the organization's budget, but rather the level of commitment of the core team to the mission of the organization and to following a systematic process for attaining sustainable funding.

Let's walk through the basic application of the Benevon Model.

It's a Circle

The model is designed as a circle. Think of this circle as an old-fashioned toy train set that goes around and around on the floor. Once your potential donors get on board, they stay on board. Your job is to tailor this model to your organization and to keep expanding it to include as many people as possible, year after year.

Step One: The Point of Entry Event

The model has four essential steps, which take each donor around the cycle. Potential donors get on the track at a Point of Entry Event, which is the engine of the entire Benevon Model and, therefore, the most critical step. This one-hour introductory tour of your mission educates and inspires people about your organization's work and opens the door for them to give you feedback and become more engaged if they choose. Even though, for some, this event will become the first step toward deeper involvement and monetary giving, the majority of guests will attend only once and never become donors. But they will still have been inspired and moved by your memorable Point of Entry Event and they will look forward to giving you feedback and telling others about your organization.

This is because, as individuals, we are emotional donors looking for rational reasons to justify our emotional decision to give.

Each guest is invited personally by a friend or someone they trust, often someone who is an official Ambassador for the organization. Guests know they are coming to a one-hour introductory session to learn about a wonderful organization. They know that they will not be asked to give money at the Point of Entry Event. They have been told in advance that they will be asked to fill out a card and that they will receive one Follow-Up Call to ask for their feedback—not their money.

A Point of Entry Event must include three components:

1. The "Facts 101" about your organization, including your three overarching areas of impact or "buckets"; the vision; and needs.
2. An "Emotional Hook" so compelling that people will never forget it.
3. A system for "capturing the names," as well as the addresses, phone numbers, and e-mail addresses of the guests, with their permission.

Your Point of Entry Event must give people a sense of how the work of your organization changes lives. This is because, as individuals, we are emotional donors looking for rational reasons to justify our emotional decision to give. This event must satisfy both the head and the heart, intertwining myth-buster facts with heartfelt stories and a clear sense of what is needed next to fill the gap.

Finally, you must be sure you have a permission-based system for capturing the contact information for every guest. Rather than tricking or manipulating guests by pretending to collect their business cards for some other purpose, you can ask people to fill out an individual guest card with their contact information because they have been told in advance what to expect.

Step Two: Follow Up and Involve

The only way you will know what your guests really thought about your organization or your Point of Entry Event is if you ask them. Therefore, the second step on the circle is making a personal Follow-Up Call within three to five days to each guest.

If you are not planning on doing a rigorous job of following up with each and every person who attends a Point of Entry Event, there is no point in having these events at all. In fact, the very first step in planning each event should be to design your follow-up system.

The purpose of the Benevon Follow-Up Call is not merely to say thank you; for that, a note would suffice. This is an interactive research call, a one-on-one focus group in which you gather critical data on each potential lifelong donor and friend. The purpose of this call is to generate an authentic dialog, which is the foundation of any lasting relationship. If you think of the people with whom you have lifelong relationships—your friends and family—you

The Follow-Up Call must be made by someone whom your guests met at the Point of Entry, not by a stranger.

will realize that these relationships are rooted in a true give-and-take dialog. It should be no different with your donors.

The Follow-Up Call must be made by someone whom your guests met at the Point of Entry, not by a stranger. This call follows a specific, five-step format that will help you easily gather the information you need.

Step One
"Thank you for coming." You certainly need to thank them. They are busy people who took the time to come to your location and give you an hour of their time to learn about something new. That is remarkable!

Step Two
Ask, "What did you think (of our tour, our organization, our issue)?" Ask enough questions to get them talking.

Step Three
Listen. This is the hardest step for most of us, and by far the most critical component of the Follow-Up Call. Stop talking and listen. In the Benevon Model, the more you listen, the more you will notice that potential donors are telling you exactly how they would like to become involved with your organization. If you are too busy talking or planning what you want to say next, you will miss these rich cues.

Step Four
If they have not already told you, ask, "Is there any way you could see yourself becoming involved with our organization?" You have no hidden agenda here. Let them tell you their own ideas, even if they do not mesh with your needs. You still need to listen and be open to considering what they offer.

You may be surprised to discover that, because people were truly inspired by your Point of Entry Event, they will naturally suggest others you should contact.

Step Five

Finally, ask, "Is there anyone else you think we should invite to a ________ (Point of Entry Event)?" Of course, when talking to your guests, you would never refer to this as a "Point of Entry Event." You will be giving the event a special name tailored for your organization.

You may be surprised to discover that, *because people were truly inspired by your Point of Entry Event*, they will naturally suggest others you should contact. Even people who are honest enough to tell you that your issue is not their top priority will often have other people for you to invite. Ask if they would contact these people directly to tell them why they came to mind and to expect your call.

Every bit of data you gather must be recorded in your database. Be sure your donor tracking system has a section for you to record and track notes about each donor contact and about your next steps.

Bless-and-Release

In the follow-up process, you are sure to come across people who will not be interested in getting more involved with your organization. The Follow-Up Call is where you can let them off the hook. Do not take this as a personal rejection or failure. Rather, put yourself in their shoes. They took the time to come to the Point of Entry Event. Yes, they were touched and impressed with what you do, but they are deeply involved in another cause that is their true passion. While they like your organization and know that you are doing good work, realistically, your group is never likely to make it to the top of their giving list.

It is as if, one by one, you are selecting the people who are going to be part of your organization's family forever. You do not want to select someone who is not really interested.

Far better to tell the truth now and let these people go, graciously. "Bless and release" them. Thank them sincerely for taking the time to attend your Point of Entry Event. If they are open enough to mention the other issue or organization they are involved with, compliment it. Honor their commitment and dedication to that cause. Do not offer to send them an envelope they can use to make a small gift to your organization. *Let them completely off the hook*. It will disarm them and distinguish you from the others.

In the long run, these people will help you in other ways, primarily by referring others or speaking highly of you in the community. Many times people have told me, "This type of program just isn't my thing. I'm deeply involved in another organization, and that's where I want to be putting my resources right now." Then, when I asked them the final question about others they know who might want to come to a Point of Entry Event, they would often say, "You should definitely call my wife (or my work colleague or my friend)! This is exactly the kind of thing they'd be interested in. In fact, I'll call them myself to tell them to expect your call." What better compliment than for a person to refer you to others and open the door for you to make that connection? You will have made a real friend just by letting someone off the hook.

Remember, this is a model for building lifelong donors—donors who are so interested in your mission that they want to stay with you for the long term. It is as if, one by one, you are selecting the people who are going to be part of your organization's family forever. You do not want to select someone who is not really interested. There are so many generous and caring individuals who truly understand and appreciate the value of what you are doing. They are the ones you are on a scouting mission to find.

The Cultivation Superhighway

Where we are headed in the Benevon Model is to the third step, where the donor will be asked for money. Notice you have not done that at either Step One, the Point of Entry Event, or at Step Two, Follow Up and Involve. You have been busy educating, inspiring, and getting to know the people who could become loyal, lifelong donors. In our model, by the time you get around to asking for money, you should be certain that each person you will be asking is ready to give.

In the old reality, "the Ask" often happened too soon, before the person had a chance to fully buy in to the mission of the organization with both their head and heart. In the new reality, there is no need for that. In fact, if you have any concern that the person may not be ready to give, don't ask yet. Trust your instincts and hold off until you know they are ready.

Asking is very much like picking the ripened, low-hanging fruit from a tree. When a person comes to your

The more contacts you have with a potential donor along the Superhighway, the more money they will give you when you ask.

Point of Entry Event, they are brand new to your organization, completely un-ripened fruit. By going through the tour, they begin to ripen, and with the Follow-Up Call, they ripen further. By the time you get around to asking them for money, it should be nothing more than "nudging the inevitable"—like easily picking a piece of fruit off a tree the moment it is ready. On the other hand, if you wait too long, what happens? The fruit becomes overripe, falls to the ground, and spoils. In other words, in the life cycle of each donor, there are perfect moments for asking for money. You have to tune your radar to those moments.

In the Benevon Model, everything along the path between Step Two, Follow Up and Involve, and Step Three, the Ask, is called the Cultivation Superhighway. The more contacts you have with a potential donor along the Superhighway, the more money they will give you when you ask. There is a direct correlation between the number of contacts with a donor and the size of the gifts received.

This should come as no surprise. Think of yourself as that donor. Imagine that an organization had already taken the time to educate and follow up with you by telephone. The more personal contacts you have had with a real individual at that organization—contacts that focus on your particular "bucket" area of interest—the more inclined you would be to make a larger gift the next time they asked. We will talk more about what we mean by personal cultivation contacts in Chapter 12.

Contacts are what ripen the fruit. The more meaningful your organization's contacts are with these individuals, the better. Donors need to know that you need them and that their contribution will make a difference in accomplishing your mission. They need to know that you will be responsive to their suggestions. In many cases, they need to know that you need them for more than their money.

Step Three: Asking for Money

There are two ways to ask for money in the Benevon Model, and most of our groups, over time, use both methods: asking one-on-one in person and asking at the Benevon Free One-Hour Ask Event.

If you have taken many people through your Point of Entry Events in the course of the year, and then followed up and involved them to their satisfaction, you may well find yourself in the enviable position of having a large number of people who are ready to be asked to make a financial contribution. In that case, the Free One-Hour Ask Event is ideal. The critical mass of true believers in the same room will produce remarkable results in just an hour. *(Note this formula: at least 40% of the guests at your Ask Event must have attended a Point of Entry in the twelve months prior to each Ask Event. We call this the "ripened fruit" percentage.)*

In addition, prior to each Ask Event, you will secure one or more significant individual gifts to be announced as a Leadership or Challenge Gift right before your attendees are asked to give money at the Ask Event.

To follow the Benevon Model properly, you will have three Unit of Service levels in one of two options.

Whether you are asking one-on-one or at the Ask Event, in the Benevon Model, every Ask must include the two essential ingredients below, which we will discuss in more detail in Chapter 13.

Multiple-Year Pledges

The first essential ingredient in asking for money using the Benevon Model is that you must ask people to become part of a Multiple-Year Giving Society by making a five-year pledge of at least $1,000 a year to support the general operational needs of the organization.

Units of Service

When asking for multiple-year pledges, it is crucial to specify the dollar levels of contribution. We call these Units of Service. They are the giving levels—the incremental chunks of unrestricted funding that one donor can support. They relate to the needs that were clearly identified at the Point of Entry and at every contact along the way.

To follow the Benevon Model properly, you will have three Unit of Service levels in one of two options. (The options are determined by your organization's recent donation history, as explained in Chapter 8). Option 1 includes three Unit of Service levels: $1,000, $5,000, and $10,000 a year for five years. Option 2 includes the similar but higher levels: $1,000, $10,000, and $25,000 a year for five years. In either case, the lowest level must be $1,000 a year (which equates to about $83 a month). Many people who truly love your work and want to be lifelong members of your organization's family can and will give at that level. In fact, many may already be giving at that level when you total up their multiple gifts each year.

The key thing to know is that these multiple-year donations fund the unrestricted operational needs of the organization; that is, they are not allocated to donor-specified programs. By the time a donor has gotten to this point, they will know and trust your organization enough to be willing to make an unrestricted gift and allow you to use it for your general operational needs. They know that someone has to pay the light bill and the salaries. They know they can look at your annual audit if they want to see exactly how the money was spent.

The pledge card for your Ask Event (see page 212) also includes a "fill-in-the-blank" box for donors to make a gift of any amount for one year or longer as well as a box for donors who wish to be contacted to share other thoughts with you.

Step Four: Introducing Others, Reconnecting Existing Donors

In the fourth step of the model, each individual member of the Multiple-Year Giving Society receives a Follow-Up Call to thank them for their gift and pledge and to ask them to introduce others to your organization by becoming an

With diligent follow-up and engagement of potential donors after each Point of Entry Event, you should be ready to put on your first Free One-Hour Ask Event at the end of the first year of implementation.

Ambassador and inviting their friends and associates to Point of Entry Events. Since your donors have been well treated as they have gone around the cycle with you, they know you will take good care of their friends. You will educate and inspire them at the Point of Entry Event, follow up personally, involve them as appropriate, or bless-and-release them if they are not interested. Your Multiple-Year Giving Society Donors will trust the organization to treat their friends with respect. Their secret hope, of course, is that their friends will fall in love with your organization too—in their own right, and for their own reasons—and become lifelong donors as well.

This step completes the first circuit around the model for a brand-new donor. You will need to allow one full year to implement the Benevon Model the first time. You should plan to have two Point of Entry Events per month for 9 to 12 months. With diligent follow-up and engagement of potential donors after each Point of Entry Event, you should be ready to put on your first Free One-Hour Ask Event at the end of the first year of implementation.

Free Feel-Good Cultivation Events

To keep your donors on the cycle, and to begin to see the power of the Benevon Model to engage major donors, every Multiple-Year Giving Society Donor is invited to two Free Feel-Good Cultivation Events during the year—also called Point of Re-Entry Events. These program-related events, which we will discuss further in Chapter 16, serve to reconnect them to the emotional impact and the facts about your work. Donors are encouraged to invite others to Free Feel-Good Cultivation Events. For new guests, this event will be their Pre-Point of Entry Event. For prior donors, the event serves to reinforce their wise investment in your organization and to deepen their interest and commitment.

Whatever the donor tells you in each Follow-Up Call determines the frequency and type of involvement this particular donor would like to have, including the timing of the next Ask.

Within three to five days after each Free Feel-Good Cultivation Event, every donor receives another one-on-one Follow-Up Call asking a few more open-ended questions and giving them the opportunity to offer suggestions for names of others to be invited to attend a Point of Entry Event and to become an Ambassador, if they wish. This in turn leads to more cultivation, more involvement, deeper permission and trust. Whatever the donor tells you in each Follow-Up Call determines the frequency and type of involvement this particular donor would like to have, including the timing of the next Ask.

Growing the Benevon Model to Sustainable Funding

After the next gift is received, another Follow-Up Call is made to say thank you, there is more conversation, and on it goes. All the while, you are looking and listening for how else this donor might want to become involved. You may even consider inviting them to take on a leadership role as a key volunteer or board member as appropriate.

Ideally, in the course of the year, you will have three or four occasions for personal, one-on-one contact with each donor. This contact can be made by your major gifts development staff person, other key staff, or one of the volunteers on your donor cultivation team. These customized contacts are nothing intrusive or artificial, but rather a natural give-and-take, directly related to the donor's "bucket" area of greatest interest or as a follow-up to one of your Free Feel-Good Cultivation Events.

By using the Benevon Model systematically over time, this simple circle becomes a spiral, with an ever-growing number of Multiple-Year Giving Society Donors. When cultivated personally, using our specific guidelines for cultivation, many of these same donors will give generously to help meet the

In fact, it is simple. But as most of our groups tell us, that doesn't mean it's easy!

needs of the organization through capital campaign contributions, endowment, or gifts restricted for funding a particular project or program, like a library or technology program.

Simple But Not Easy

It all sounds so simple. Four steps around a circle: Point of Entry, Follow Up and Involve, Ask for Money, and Introduce Others. Launch a Multiple-Year Giving Society, fill the pipeline, collect the cash and pledges every year. In fact, it is simple. But as most of our groups tell us, that doesn't mean it's easy!

Now that you understand the basics of the Benevon Model for Sustainable Funding and have reconnected to your deep passion for the mission of your organization, you are ready to begin the 12-step implementation process.

CHAPTER 4

STEP ONE: ENGAGING YOUR BOARD

Most groups tell us there is a direct correlation between their success with implementing the Benevon Model and the level of engagement of their board members. In other words, as the Benevon Model takes hold and grows roots in the daily life of your organization, you should naturally find your current and former board members becoming more involved in the work of the board and the organization, or offering to step off the board to make room for new people who may have been introduced to your organization at a Point of Entry Event or an Ask Event and want to become more involved—at the board level.

Much has been written and said about the roles for board members today, their fiduciary responsibilities and effective models for board governance. Clearly, the board's first role is to govern the organization. Yet that is often not how it feels to board members. While they may have been recruited for their particular area of expertise, influence, or contacts, board members know that sooner or later they will be asked to do the dreaded thing the organization needs most: fundraising. Most often this looks like buying or selling tickets to the organization's fundraising social events and soliciting their friends and colleagues for money, either by letter or in person.

Before she has even been oriented to the basics of being on the board, the new member is being asked to do the part she dreaded most.

The typical scenario looks something like this:

The nominating committee of your board starts by identifying the categories of expertise needing to be filled on the board. For example, you may be looking for someone with experience in human resources, real estate, finance, public relations, or fundraising. Each potential board member is checked out thoroughly, courted, and then invited to join the board. Your organization is thrilled when they accept.

Each new board member reads over the written agreement listing what is expected of them. You even make sure they see all the fine print about their fundraising responsibilities. Perhaps your organization has a minimum giving expectation for the board, or a "give, get, or get off" policy. Whatever your expectations, you do your best to communicate them clearly to each new board member before they agree to serve.

Now, as your fresh and eager new recruit arrives at one of her first board meetings, ready to fill the "CPA slot," for example, one of the main agenda items is, of course, fundraising. It just happens to be the time of year for the big annual banquet, golf tournament, or fund drive. Before she has even been oriented to the basics of being on the board, the new member is being asked to do the part she dreaded most. Yes, she did know this was coming eventually, and she did agree to help. So she takes a deep breath and scans her address book for her five closest friends or colleagues who cannot refuse her. After all, she has helped them in similar times of need.

Think for a moment about how it feels for her friends to be on the receiving end of one of those Asks. In most cases, those friends cannot say no. Their relationship with your board member, whether professional or personal, would make it very awkward to refuse. In their minds, their contribution is more akin to a business expense.

The times I have been "strong-armed" by my friends on other boards, I have had to say yes. But as soon as my friend goes off that board, I stop giving to that organization.

The times I have been "strong-armed" by my friends on other boards, I have had to say yes. But as soon as my friend goes off that board, I stop giving to that organization. It is not because it was a bad organization. On the contrary, they were almost certainly doing very good work. Had they taken the time to educate and cultivate me personally, I could have become a lifelong supporter in my own right. But in their minds, I was my friend's contact so they left me alone, not wanting to intrude.

In terms of their love of fundraising, a random sample of board members will pretty much mirror the larger population. In other words, fundraising is just not everyone's favorite activity. The same folks who may be brilliant at strategic planning, finance, or human resources may not feel they have the knack for fundraising. Remember, you did not initially recruit all of them for their fundraising expertise. That would be akin to asking all board members to be responsible for reviewing the annual audit in detail or securing the next piece of real estate for the organization.

On the other hand, there is a portion of the population that actually likes to ask others for money, especially when they are asking on behalf of an organization they truly believe in. Those are the board members you intentionally recruited to fill the fundraising slots. You put them on the development committee. At the proper point in the fundraising/cultivation cycle, these board members will be of great help in asking for money, but not until potential donors have attended a Point of Entry Event, received a Follow-Up Call, and been cultivated sufficiently to be ready to be asked.

As most of us have learned the hard way, *pressuring board members to do fundraising does not work*. Even if they say they will make those three calls to ask people for money, many never seem to get around to it. For some, this pressure leads to poor attendance at meetings. Eventually they withdraw or resign from the board feeling guilty, frustrated, or resentful.

The fantasy of the magical fundraising board that will do all the work and raise all the money is just that: a fantasy.

Board Envy: The Ideal Fundraising Board

Most nonprofits aspire to have their board become a "fundraising board," either because they think that is what an ideal board should be, or because they think it would handle their fundraising needs forever. They berate themselves for not having this ideal fundraising board. I refer to this as "board envy," and it is not rooted in any reality I have ever seen.

When you pull back the curtain from those well-established organizations with "fundraising boards" that are the envy of every other group, you will find a team of dedicated, hard-working staff who coordinate the process of strategically cultivating each donor and engaging volunteer board members at every step of the way, including the ultimate Ask.

The fantasy of the magical fundraising board that will do all the work and raise all the money is just that: a fantasy. Those organizations with "ideal" fundraising boards have a systematic plan for how they grow and cultivate relationships with donors. While they involve their board members strategically in the cultivation and asking process, they certainly don't rely on their board members to save the day.

We work with many groups that have well-established fundraising programs, including groups that are already raising many millions of dollars each year before they come to our workshops. They often tell us they still do not feel they have a system for keeping their board members engaged. They experience board burnout and turnover, just like the small and mid-sized organizations do. They use our model as a mission-centered strategy for ongoing donor—and board—engagement.

If you are truly committed to leaving the legacy of self-sustaining funding, there is no better place to start than with your board. Rather than distracting your focus and wasting time comparing your board to others, get to work on specific strategies for keeping your board engaged.

Above all, treat your board members as if they are your most cherished major donors. That is the Benevon Golden Rule.

The Benevon Golden Rule

Above all, treat your board members as if they are your most cherished major donors. That is the Benevon Golden Rule.

It sounds simple enough, yet when you scan through the list of your board members one by one—if you tell the truth—there may be a few members whom you've already written off in your mind, either because they are annoying or troublesome to you in some way, or because you have predetermined that they do not have the capacity to become a major donor. That is a violation of the Benevon Golden Rule.

Compare that to how you think about your list of major donors, at whatever dollar level you define as "major." Think of all the special things you do or try to do for those donors—special events, letters, calls, and meetings. Think about the respect and humility you bring to each interaction, regardless of that donor's quirky personality. You have a great deal of tolerance for your major donors, knowing their capacity to give.

Why, then, would you treat your board members differently? These are people who are giving their own time to do something you invited them to do, to serve on your board. That is a great gift unto itself.

Furthermore, the statistics show that 90% of people who volunteer in America also give money. That doesn't mean they necessarily give money to the same organizations where they volunteer. It just means that "volunteering" people are also "giving" people.

And here, in your board members, you have the most dedicated volunteers. Why not assume they will become your most passionate major donors? Even if they do not have the capacity to give a large gift now, odds are they will be making charitable gifts at the end of their lives to one or more organizations. Where else would they rather give that money than to an organization that has treated them well throughout the years—an organization whose work they

Here are three easy ways for every board member to participate in the fundraising process, without ever having to ask anyone for money themselves...

know and love and perhaps has benefited them or their families personally?

What systems do you have for cultivating and engaging your major donors? You have a plan for talking to them several times a year, personally and face-to-face. You invite them to special mission-focused Free Feel-Good Cultivation Events each year. You continue to deepen your relationship with them, very intentionally, finding out at every opportunity how else they might like to become involved, what more they need from the organization, and who else they might want to introduce.

These are the same sorts of systems you will want to put in place for your board members.

Three Roles for Board Members

The fastest route to sanity and satisfaction is to accept the 20-60-20 rule when it comes to fundraising and your board members. That is, 20% of the board will enjoy being involved in fundraising, 60% will be neutral about it, and the remaining 20% will want nothing to do with it.

Here are three easy ways for every board member to participate in the fundraising process, without ever having to ask anyone for money themselves:

- *Serve as Ambassadors by inviting people to Point of Entry Events*. If your board members did nothing more than this, they would be making an enormous contribution to the future of your organization. They can agree to be the board member "host of the month" for a regularly scheduled Point of Entry Event and then invite a few people to attend that event. Or they can host a private event just for their friends, business colleagues, or civic group.

What would it take for your board to more closely resemble your image of the "ideal" board?

- *Thank donors for gifts*. Ask your board members to telephone recent happy individual donors just to thank them. Not all board members will want to do this, but once a few of them report at the next board meeting on how rewarding the experience was, others may offer to jump in.

- *Give money themselves*. You need to be able to tell your community that 100% of your board members give money personally to your organization, regardless of the amount. Many board members will make their gift at the annual Ask Event. Others may choose to be part of a pooled Leadership or Challenge Gift. We do not recommend setting a minimum gift expectation for board members. If you cultivate and ask each board member individually for their gift, you will be treating each board member as if they will become your most cherished major donor, thereby abiding by the Benevon Golden Rule.

Top Ten Checklist: Involving Your Board in the Fundraising Process

How does your board stack up? Here is a series of questions that will get to the truth about how you are doing at involving your board. Write down your answers to each question below.

1. When it comes to fundraising, what are your biggest concerns about your board? What more would you like your board members to be doing? What would it take for your board to more closely resemble your image of the "ideal" board?

What percentage of your total board members would you rate as truly passionate about your work?

2. What percentage of your total board members would you rate as truly passionate about your work? Do the math. The sooner you tell the truth about this percentage, the sooner you can get to work.

3. What percentage of your total board members understand the Benevon Model and are eager to participate in its implementation—not just how many have heard of the model or nod their heads pleasantly when you discuss Point of Entry Events and the Ask Event? Rather, what percentage truly understand the power of the Benevon Model to build long-term sustainable funding, which is something most board members would love to leave as a legacy?

4. What percentage of total board members have attended your organization's Point of Entry Event? Even if board members think they know everything there is to know about your organization, they will learn something new and personally experience the power of your mission. Tell them in advance that you need their advice and feedback.

5. What percentage of your board members have invited others to attend Point of Entry Events? Some groups make this a standard part of board participation, going so far as to have board members sign an agreement to participate at a certain level, for instance, to attend at least one Point of Entry Event per year, or to have a minimum number of guests throughout the year, or to become an official Ambassador, which requires having at least 10 guests attend over the course of one year.

If your CEO and board chair were to do an annual Treasure Map Interview with each of your board members, that would send a powerful message that each board member is very important to your organization.

6. What percentage of your board members have been involved in thanking donors? What have they said about it afterwards? Do you give them an opportunity to share these experiences at board meetings?

7. What percentage of your board members give money to the organization, personally? Your goal here should be 100% participation with no minimum dollar requirement.

8. Have you completed a Treasure Map Interview with each board member once a year? These simple Treasure Map Interview questions (Chapter 6) are very powerful. If your CEO and board chair were to do an annual Treasure Map Interview with each of your board members, that would send a powerful message that each board member is very important to your organization.

   Treasure Map Interviews give your board members an opportunity to talk to you and, even more importantly, give you an opportunity to listen to them, which again sends the message that you value them. Furthermore, if you pay close attention to what they are telling you in these annual interviews, you will see what has changed in their life circumstances and priorities in the past year, what lights them up most about your work, and how you can involve them in precisely those areas, just as you would cultivate a major donor.

This new level of engagement for each board member isn't going to happen automatically. It takes someone to drive it, step by step.

9. What is your plan to increase or retread your board members' passion? This new level of engagement for each board member isn't going to happen automatically. It takes someone to drive it, step by step. Just as you would develop a cultivation plan for each major donor, you need a similar step-by-step plan for cultivating each board member. This will be a series of personalized contacts, each focusing on the board member's particular area of interest, which you will know well. Each subsequent contact is driven by the board member's request during the prior contact.

10. Do you have an annual board fundraising retreat where each board member signs an annual board agreement, outlining the options and requirements for participation?

Annual Board Fundraising Retreat

To keep the Benevon Model fresh as board members come and go, I recommend you hold an annual board fundraising retreat. Here is the proposed 90-minute agenda for this retreat, which can be used as the agenda for a stand-alone event, a special board meeting, or as part of an all-day retreat that may include other topics.

BOARD RETREAT SAMPLE AGENDA (90 MINUTES)

Item	Presenter	Time
1. Welcome and Introductions	Executive Director/ Board Chair	5 min.
2. Do the "Passion Retread" exercise: have each board member say why they chose to volunteer with the organization.	Executive Director/ Board Chair	15 min.
3. Share the legacy goals your team has developed (Chapter 7). (At some point this should be discussed and agreed upon by the organization leadership.)	Development Director	5 min.
4. Review customized Benevon Model diagram. Show how the model works.	Board Member	10 min.
5. Review financial goals: Leadership/Challenge Gift: $ __________ Sponsorship: $ __________ Total Ask Event $__________ Major Gifts: $__________ Capital: $__________ Endowment: $__________	Board Member	10 min.
6. Introduce the Ambassador concept.	Board Member	5 min.
7. Make a quick Treasure Map with the board (or walk them through the one you have already done). Show them the list of potential Ambassadors you have developed.	Team Leader	15 min.
8. Have each board member make a Personal Treasure Map and identify at least 15 people they could invite to a Point of Entry Event.	Team Leader	5 min.
9. Review the Board Agreement document.	Board Member	10 min.
10. Discussion/Q & A	Executive Director/ Board Chair	10 min.

Let's walk through this agenda step by step, because it includes several critical elements that can be used at other times of the year as well.

As the stories spill out, members of the group will rediscover their connection to the organization.

Passion Retread Exercise (15 minutes)

After the welcome and introductions, which should take no longer than five minutes, the first item on the agenda sets the tone. The Passion Retread exercise, which I described in Chapter 2, is easy to do, non-threatening, and guaranteed to connect people to their passion for your work—and to each other—very quickly. That's why we put it first on the agenda. Once people are in touch with why they are giving their time to your group, they have a great deal more compassion for one another and can focus on the work at hand.

Here's how it works. Have your facilitator, board chair, or executive director ask people to think about this question: "What is so special about the work of this organization that makes you want to give your time to it?"

Then go around the group, person by person, and ask each board member to share their response. You'll find that some of the stories are very personal and moving, while others may be touching and amusing. As the stories spill out, members of the group will rediscover their connection to the organization. At the same time, participants will gain a deeper respect for and connection to each other, even the more challenging members.

In the end, all who participate in this exercise will have new energy and enthusiasm for telling the story of the organization to the community. They will be reminded of just how important the work of this organization is and why they want to serve on the board.

Legacy Goals (5 minutes)

Next, the board member who is responsible for your organization's implementation of the Benevon Model shares the short-term and long-term sustainable funding goals your team

Review the size of your Leadership or Challenge Gift, sponsorship, and total dollars to be raised in cash and pledges from the Ask Event.

has established with the rest of the board. How much money are you aiming to raise, by when, and what is the impact that funding will have on your organization and on the community? We will discuss this in more detail in Chapter 7.

Review Customized Benevon Model Diagram (10 minutes)

Walk the board through the basics of the Benevon Model. Groups often have this part of the agenda presented by a board member or former board member who has served on their Sustainable Funding Team (Chapter 5) and who sees the long-term merit of the model.

An alternative to having someone explain the Benevon Model in person is showing the board one of our free online videos, although this will take longer than 10 minutes. Tell your board members the name of your Point of Entry Event and show them where the Ask Event lives on the cycle, so that they see it is just one step in a four-step circular process that spirals up to major gifts and endowment.

Review Financial Goals (10 minutes)

The same board member who is leading your Sustainable Funding Team should review your annual financial goals here, tell them the date of your next Ask Event and, using our formulas, the number of Ambassadors and Point of Entry guests you will need to have by a specific date. Review the size of your Leadership or Challenge Gift, sponsorship, and total dollars to be raised in cash and pledges from the Ask Event. This is also a good time to mention any other fundraising goals that the organization has for the year, including major gifts, capital, or endowment.

Ideally, the board chair leads this part of the agenda, guiding people through the written agreement in their packets listing the optional and required agreements for serving on the board.

Introduce Ambassador Concept (5 minutes)
Explain the critical role of Ambassadors in engaging new people. Show the job description for a volunteer Ambassador (Chapter 6) and invite every board member to become an Ambassador if they choose, but only after they have attended your sizzling Point of Entry Event.

Make a quick Treasure Map (Chapter 6). Let them identify groups in the community they feel would want to know you better. Show them the list of Ambassadors you have developed and invite them again to become an Ambassador if they have not done so already.

Personal Treasure Map (5 minutes)
Have each board member make a personal Treasure Map (Chapter 6) of the people in their lives who would naturally want to attend your Point of Entry Event. Ask them to make a list of at least 15 of those people. This list can become their guest list if they agree to be an Ambassador and ultimately a Table Captain at the Ask Event.

When combined with the many groups on your organization's Treasure Map, these personal Treasure Maps of your board members, collectively, could fill many Point of Entry Events and ensure a high percentage of ripened fruit at your Ask Event.

Review Board Agreement (10 minutes)
Ideally, the board chair leads this part of the agenda, guiding people through the written agreement in their packets listing the optional and required agreements for serving on the board.

Here is the Sample Board Agreement we recommend, which you would customize for your board.

SAMPLE BOARD AGREEMENT

Our board is committed to attaining financial sustainability. We have adopted the Benevon Model. Over the next year, I agree to (check as many as you like):

- ❑ 1. Attend our annual board sustainable funding retreat
- ❑ 2. Be an Ambassador: Invite 10 people to our ________(Point of Entry Event)
- ❑ 3. Attend at least one _________(Point of Entry Event) as board "host"
- ❑ 4. Attend our ____________ (Ask Event)
- ❑ 5. Be a Table Captain at our _________(Ask Event) and fill a table of 10 with at least half of my guests having attended a prior ___________(Point of Entry Event)
- ❑ 6. Make thank-you calls to donors
- ❑ 7. Attend at least one donor cultivation event as board representative

I understand that our board has committed to 100% board giving so that we can tell other funders and supporters in our community that 100% of our board gives. Therefore, I further agree to:

- ❑ 8. Make a financial contribution (usually required)

Discussion/Q&A (10 minutes)

Be sure to allow time for even the quietest of board members to express themselves. Try to get feedback from every board member.

To Summarize

Your board members are volunteers. They are a gift to your organization. Treat each board member as you would treat every other significant major donor. Give them the one-on-one, personal attention that honors their involvement. In every interaction, share a human story or recent example of the impact of your work. Show them the utmost respect and care. Then they will want to become your most stalwart lifelong donors. In addition to giving, they will introduce their friends and colleagues who, in turn, will become loyal lifelong donors.

CHAPTER 5

STEP TWO: BUILDING YOUR CORE TEAM

The most reliable predictor of an organization's successful implementation of the Benevon Model is the presence of a strong and diverse, self-sustaining team of people to diligently manage and carry out each step of the process.

Even if your organization already has a sophisticated development staff, I believe it truly does a disservice to a nonprofit organization—long term—not to engage more people in the process right from the start. Even if you attend our programs and are serious about building sustainable funding for an organization you love, you will not be able to do it alone. You need a team.

We have watched many a superstar development person or major gifts officer adopt the Benevon Model singlehandedly without ever getting the deeper buy-in of the executive director, CEO, board, or other key volunteers. It is painful to observe how hard that one person works to achieve financial success the first year.

The second year is where we see these superstars become frustrated. Because the others in the organization never truly understood that the Benevon Model is a process for building sustainable funding from individual donors, they focus only on the one aspect of the model they witnessed, the Ask Event, leaving the staff feeling unappreciated, burned out, and ready to move on.

The primary focus of this team is to build one-on-one relationships with donors and to tend those relationships over time.

When that sole implementer leaves, no one will be left behind to cultivate and involve your new Multiple-Year Donors, or help sustain those relationships so they will want to stay with you for years to come. No one will be there to expand the reach of your Point of Entry Events to other groups within the community. Rather than nurturing the process so that it becomes a strong, deeply-rooted, fruit-bearing tree, the low-hanging fruit will have been picked and the tree will have been left unwatered.

Without painting too bleak a picture, suffice it to say that lasting, systemic change within a nonprofit organization cannot be achieved by one person alone. Attaining sustainable funding requires a self-refreshing, dedicated team of people representing different roles within the organization—staff, board, and volunteers—who commit to customizing the Benevon Model and implementing it, faithfully, over time.

Building Your Sustainable Funding Team

The nonprofit groups we train and coach often refer to this group as their Sustainable Funding Team. The primary focus of this team is to build one-on-one relationships with donors and to tend those relationships over time. Most organizations do not have such a team already in place. The nearest thing they have is a development committee typically composed of busy board members who were recruited to plan special events or solicit individual donors.

Ideal Team Make-Up

Your Sustainable Funding Team must be a cross-functional team of five to seven people: staff, board, and volunteers. Our ideal team configuration consists of two staff, two or three board members, and two or three volunteers. Staff members must include the executive director and, if your organization has one, a development director. Board members should

Aim to have as much diversity as possible on your team, including age, gender, ethnicity, and community reach.

include the board chair or vice chair, the board development committee chair, and one other board member who is passionate about engaging the community in your mission. Volunteers may include former board members, program volunteers like tutors and mentors, and volunteers who have helped with prior fundraising events. Aim to have as much diversity as possible on your team, including age, gender, ethnicity, and community reach. *This dedicated, carefully crafted team of people is essential to your success.*

Staffing

While preferable, it is not essential to have a dedicated full-time staff member assigned to the Benevon Model the first year of implementation. If you have a staff member who can devote up to half time the first year, that staff member should serve as the Team Leader. If you have no dedicated staff member the first year, then one of your volunteer team members must serve as the Team Leader, coordinating the various responsibilities of each team member.

Most groups find after their success with the Benevon Model the first year, they are ready to invest in a full-time staff person to manage their implementation of the model in the second year. This person becomes the Team Leader, responsible for ensuring that each team member is fulfilling their duties.

This does not necessarily mean you will need to add a new staff position to the budget the second year. Most groups find, after experiencing first-year success with the Benevon Model, their priorities shift away from some of the more labor-intensive fundraising activities that have been consuming limited staff time. They are able to bring onto the team one or more of their dedicated special events or annual fund staff members who have a real knack for the relationship-building aspects of the model, thereby saving the cost of adding staff positions.

A second sub-team develops, usually in the third year, to focus solely on donor cultivation and one-on-one asking.

Two Teams

As the model is implemented over time, the Sustainable Funding Team subdivides into two teams. The first team is perpetually focused on filling the pipeline with new potential donors. This team oversees Ambassadors, Points of Entry, Follow-Up Calls and the cultivation of guests up to and including their attendance at the Benevon Free One-Hour Ask Event.

A second sub-team develops, usually in the third year, to focus solely on donor cultivation and one-on-one asking. This team's work begins after the Ask Event, growing and deepening the relationship with each donor. They will accomplish this primarily through one-on-one cultivation visits and by inviting donors to become Ambassadors, attend Free Feel-Good Cultivation Events, and participate in other committees and projects of special interest, leading up to the next major gifts Ask.

Choosing Team Members

We spend a great deal of time helping groups put together an effective team. I don't think we have ever had a group call us and say they already have a perfect team in place and are ready to come into our Benevon 101 Workshop and Coaching Program. Rather, most groups initially feel they do not have five to seven people who would want to be involved with this, regardless of whether they are board members, staff, or volunteers.

This feeling is normal, so don't be discouraged about finding excellent team members. Look over your group's Treasure Map (Chapter 6) for possible team members who are right under your nose. Former board members are my first choice for the ideal team member. If they were strong, contributing board members for many years, people who loved telling other people about your work, and if they left in good standing, their passion is likely still there for the organization.

Choose people who are upbeat, fun to work with, organized, and who do what they say they will do.

Serving on the Sustainable Funding Team is a different type of commitment than serving on the board. Rather than carrying the responsibility of governing and overseeing the entire operation, first and foremost a team member needs to be an Ambassador for your organization in the community. Therefore, choose the people who love talking about your organization and who are naturally going to do that, whether they are on your board or not. Choose people who are upbeat, fun to work with, organized, and who do what they say they will do. Choose the people who will enjoy doing this and will not need a lot of tending. Think long-term sustainability: choose the people you would trust to carry the Benevon Model forward even after you are gone.

Team Member Job Description

The specific responsibilities of each team member will vary depending on that person's role on the team as well as their interests and strengths. This team member job description lists the primary responsibilities of most team members.

Team Member Job Description

1. Attend a Benevon Introductory Session or watch the free online video describing the Benevon Model
2. Attend one initial Point of Entry Event
3. Be an Ambassador and bring at least 10 friends each year to a Point of Entry Event
4. Make a Personal Treasure Map twice a year and add names to the list of potential Point of Entry attendees
5. Make thank-you phone calls and invitation calls as requested
6. Attend Free Feel-Good Cultivation Events and bring others
7. Take on other special roles on the team as desired (e.g., be a greeter at Point of Entry Events)

The first year, we say it takes an average of 20 to 30 hours per week for a team of five to seven people to collectively implement the Benevon Model.

8. Attend the monthly Benevon team meetings
9. Serve as a Table Captain at the Ask Event and fill a table with nine other people who have attended a prior Point of Entry Event

Time Commitment

What sort of time commitment will this take? The first year, we say it takes an average of 20 to 30 hours per week for a team of five to seven people to collectively implement the Benevon Model. That means the average team member can expect to spend two to five hours per week on this.

That being said, other than the time each team member devotes to being an effective Ambassador, the 20 to 30 hours per week your team spends on implementing the Benevon Model will probably not be divided evenly among the team members. Some will do more in the beginning—perhaps they will plan and manage the Point of Entry Events. Others may be involved in the middle of the process, in the Follow Up and Cultivation phase of the model, and others may step up for the Ask Event or for the ongoing tending of your new donors.

As the process evolves, team members may increase their level of involvement. Do not be surprised when team members become reconnected to the work of the organization and take on a greater role on the team.

Start by asking for a minimum of a one-year commitment to serve on the team. That is as much as most people will be willing to commit to at first, especially for something that is still relatively unknown. Let people know that you hope they will become so engaged in the process that they will want to continue on after the first year.

Groups in our longer-term programs have team members who have been with them for upwards of five years, including long-time CEOs and current and former board members.

Much like the Ask Event donor who chooses to make a multiple-year financial pledge to your organization, many team members will recommit at a more personal level to be part of the team, year after year.

Once the team has defined the game plan for achieving sustainable funding, team members will see a clear pathway and know the steps to be taken. You may be surprised to see how many will want to stick around to be part of the process.

Much like the Ask Event donor who chooses to make a multiple-year financial pledge to your organization, many team members will recommit at a more personal level to be part of the team, year after year. This, in turn, attracts others. Rather than struggling to fill an empty "slot" on a team, you will be blessed with an abundance of wonderful contenders. After all, who wouldn't want to be part of a winning team dedicated to the financial sustainability of an organization they are passionate about?

Choosing Your Team Leader

The Team Leader has a unique role—to coordinate the team's efforts, not to do all the work! We recommend that the Team Leader be the person who is responsible for the fund development process within the organization. Usually this is a paid staff member, ideally the development director if the organization has one.

The biggest challenge for Team Leaders is to delegate tasks to people who are often higher in the organization's hierarchy, such as their executive director or esteemed board members.

As the team meets regularly to update their progress, people's enthusiasm builds, and people naturally take on parts of the process that they enjoy. This allows the Team Leader to function more like an orchestra conductor. The key is starting with team members who really want to be on the team, who care deeply about the organization, and will roll up their sleeves and do the work.

The best way to keep your team members feeling connected is to make sure they attend one of your sizzling Point of Entry Events at least once a year.

The Team Leader's responsibilities include:

- Coordinating the organization's implementation of the Benevon Model
- Managing the team to meet deadlines and complete assigned tasks
- Ensuring that all data is captured in the database tracking system
- Personally taking on or delegating all tasks needed to fulfill each element of the Benevon implementation plan
- Recruiting and grooming the next Team Leader, when the time comes

Keeping Team Members Passionate and Feeling Appreciated

The best way to keep your team members feeling connected is to make sure they attend one of your sizzling Point of Entry Events at least once a year. Many will do that naturally, in the course of serving as an Ambassador and inviting their friends to attend.

Ask team members to talk about their experiences on the team with their fellow board members, staff, or volunteers. Let them help you get people excited about the process.

Showcase their work at board meetings, volunteer-appreciation events, and certainly at your Free One-Hour Ask Event. While recognition is not the main reason your team members are participating, everyone appreciates being thanked, and it will inspire others to get involved.

Do not worry as some of your team members naturally cycle off the team.

Turnover: Building a Self-Sustaining Team

Over time, our groups have streamlined the team member job responsibilities so as to distribute the work more evenly and continually add new team members. For example, one organization we work with has a sub-team leader for each step of the model—Point of Entry Events, Follow Up, the Ask Event, cultivation, and one-on-one asking. That way, as new, qualified, passionate people come forward, they can groom them as team members or sub-team leaders, providing a sustainable system for refreshing each role on the team and allowing people to step off after several years of service, if they so choose.

The best time to plan for those transitions is after each year's Ask Event. Meet as a team to celebrate your success and debrief the year's results and lessons learned. Look ahead to the next phase of implementation—be it cultivation, asking for major gifts, or planning Free Feel-Good Cultivation Events. Ask people how they would like to be involved moving forward. Encourage people to stay on the team, so they can have the satisfaction of seeing the model grow over time.

This is also the time to "bless and release" those who do not want to continue in a formal role on your team. Be sure to find out how they would like to stay involved, for example as VIP guests at your Ask Event. Do not worry as some of your team members naturally cycle off the team. If you have been following the Benevon Model diligently, you'll be able to refresh your team with some of the passionate new people the model will have attracted—including new board members.

Now that you are equipped with a supportive board and hard-working team, let's turn to one of the most critical and challenging aspects of implementing the Benevon Model: how to ensure that every Point of Entry Event is filled with interested and enthusiastic guests.

CHAPTER 6

STEP THREE: START WHERE YOU ARE, BUILD ON WHAT YOU HAVE

Once you adopt the Benevon Model for Sustainable Funding in earnest, your primary focus will be on keeping your Point of Entry Events filled with a steady stream of new guests. In this chapter, we will discuss the two programs you will need for accomplishing this: Ambassadors and Know-Thy-Donor/Know-Thy-Volunteer.

Creating An Ambassador Program

Ambassadors are the people who are so passionate about your work they will happily invite others to attend your Point of Entry Events. If you can develop a system for recruiting and managing a self-renewing group of Ambassadors, the job of implementing the Benevon Model becomes a lot more enjoyable and successful!

There are only two requirements for being an Ambassador: having passion for the mission of your organization, and the ability to have at least 10 guests attend your Point of Entry Events over the course of the next few months or, at most, one year. But before you can invite these potential Ambassadors, you must identify who they are. What will help you to do this is establishing a gold-standard attribute list and extending your reach with a Treasure Map.

Regardless of their official role with your organization today, these people feel as if your work is their work, they feel as if they are part of your family.

The Gold Standard

The best way to identify potential Ambassadors is to first clarify the attributes of an ideal "gold-standard" Ambassador. Using the chart provided later in this chapter, make a quick list of the top 5 to 10 people who most love your organization and will say yes to pretty much anything you ever ask them to do. These are the people who follow through on what they promise, keep in touch, tell their friends about you, and offer to help you on special projects, for example. For these people, your organization is at the top of their list. You may notice that some, but perhaps not all, of your board members belong on this list. Also, some of your volunteers and past board members may belong on the list, although their current affiliation with your organization is loose at best. Regardless of their official role with your organization today, these people feel as if your work is their work, they feel as if they are part of your family. Do not screen this list by wealth or contacts. The only screening criteria should be their demonstrated passion and follow-through.

Now, step back and look at your list. What are the common attributes of the people on your list? Write them down on a separate list. Usually people list things like: they always show up, they return our calls, they tell their friends about us, they ask how else they can help, they do what they say they're going to do, they have a personal connection to our mission, they feel like insiders, we can talk openly with them about what's really going on.

Think about those attributes. Notice that the list does not necessarily include giving money. The people who fit this description are the natural champions for your mission, your ideal potential Ambassadors.

These are the gold-standard attributes that you will be looking for as you recruit all future Ambassadors. Keep one or two of these people in mind as you expand your list of possible Ambassadors to remind you of the qualities you are looking

Your Treasure Map will help you to recognize those natural supporters who are right under your nose.

for. Your goal is to find and develop as many more people as possible who have these same types of attributes who will in turn invite others to your Points of Entry. *Do not lower your standards.*

Creating Your Organization's Treasure Map

Now let's see how you can expand your list of potential gold-standard Ambassadors—that is, those people who would want to be invited to a Point of Entry Event and who also have the capacity to introduce others. This begins with the invaluable Treasure Map.

We use the term "Treasure Map" because it illustrates the unique treasure around your organization right now. No other organization's Treasure Map will be the same as yours. That's because you have distinct networks, as you will see. Your Treasure Map will help you to recognize those natural supporters who are right under your nose. These are the loyal volunteers, donors, and friends of the organization who may be wondering when you are going to finally notice them. As you create your Treasure Map, avoid the temptation to rely only on people with wealth and social status. Include everyone and brainstorm away!

Building a Treasure Map is best done with a team of people—ideally, the same team that will be involved in implementing the Benevon Model within your organization over the next year. The more diverse your team members, the more diverse the Treasure Map. At some point, you will want to complete this exercise with your board members as well. One tip: if you are the person who will be leading the group through the process, be sure to practice it first with a small group of staff members, family, or friends.

Get out a large piece of paper and colored markers and lead your team through the process. Begin by drawing a small circle in the center of the page. Put the name of your organization in the center of the circle.

TREASURE MAP
GROUPS AND ORGANIZATIONS

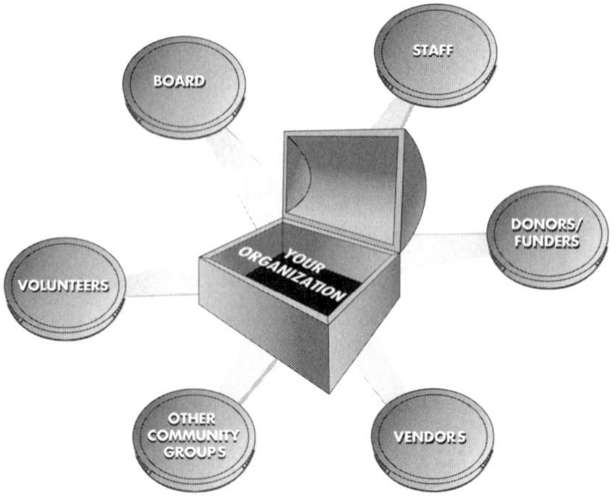

Then surround your organization, like the spokes on a wheel, with all the other groups you come in contact with on a regular basis. Start with groups such as your board, staff, volunteers, donors and funders, vendors, and other groups in the community that you interact with regularly.

You may be able to further subdivide groups; for example, your board or staff might be divided into former board members, former board presidents, founding board members, and so on. Your donors may be subcategorized into special event donors, direct-mail donors, lapsed donors, or former capital campaign donors. Similarly, your volunteers may be subdivided by the type of projects they are involved with. United Way, for example, has many substrata of "loaned executive" volunteers—depending on the industry they came from or the industry they will be soliciting. Red Cross volunteers may be subcategorized as blood volunteers, disaster volunteers, health and safety volunteers, and so on.

Take the time to brainstorm as many groups as you can think of. You can lump all the civic groups and clubs under one category. All the other community organizations you interact with may be categorized as one group or you may choose to subdivide them into subgroups such as law enforcement, schools, other arts organizations, etc.

The more detail you can put into the Treasure Map as you list these groups, the more you will be able to target their specific resources and their self-interest in the later steps of the Treasure Map process.

TREASURE MAP
ABUNDANT RESOURCES

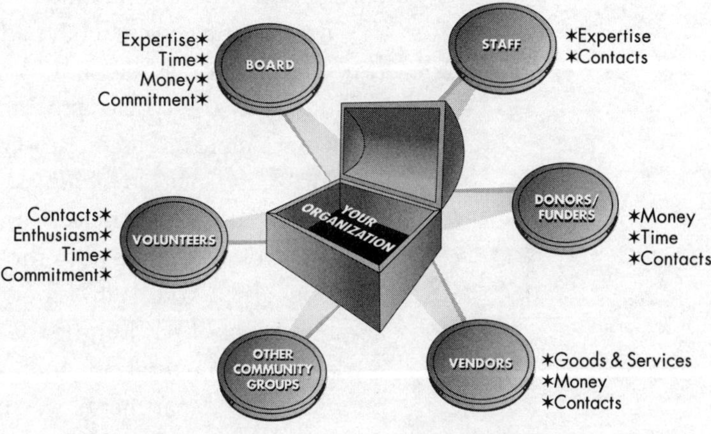

Resources in Abundance

Go back to each group or sub-group and list the resources that each of these groups has in abundance. Why? Because the Benevon Model is an abundance-based model of fundraising. It presumes people will naturally want to give that which they have in abundance.

Most of us do not like saying no; it makes us feel mean and uncaring. People would rather say yes when you ask them. It is much easier for them to say yes if you are asking them to give you something you know they already have in excess. For some people you may not know what that is, but it usually doesn't take long to find out when you think about who you could ask.

List the abundant resources of each group on your Treasure Map, such as your board, staff, and volunteers. Take the time to look closely at each group or subgroup. You will notice that their resources may be different. For example, your board in general might have an abundance of passion, commitment, expertise, contacts, and money. Yet your former board presidents may have additional resources, such as a long-term commitment to your organization, or certain connections in the community.

Your volunteers might have an abundance of time, expertise, connections, and money as well. When you categorize volunteers by the type of program they are involved with, you will see more resources. Reading tutors, for example, may have an abundance of teaching skills, an abundance of contacts in the educational field, or an abundance of passion and personal stories to share from the people they have tutored.

How about your staff? They have dedicated time and an abundance of passion, firsthand stories about the good work of your organization, and expertise. Staff in different programs and departments will have different stories and different connections. Volunteer coordinators will have had direct contact with volunteer tutors. Program directors may have more contact with other nonprofit organizations in the community.

Take the time to do this with each group. Consider what resources they have in abundance.

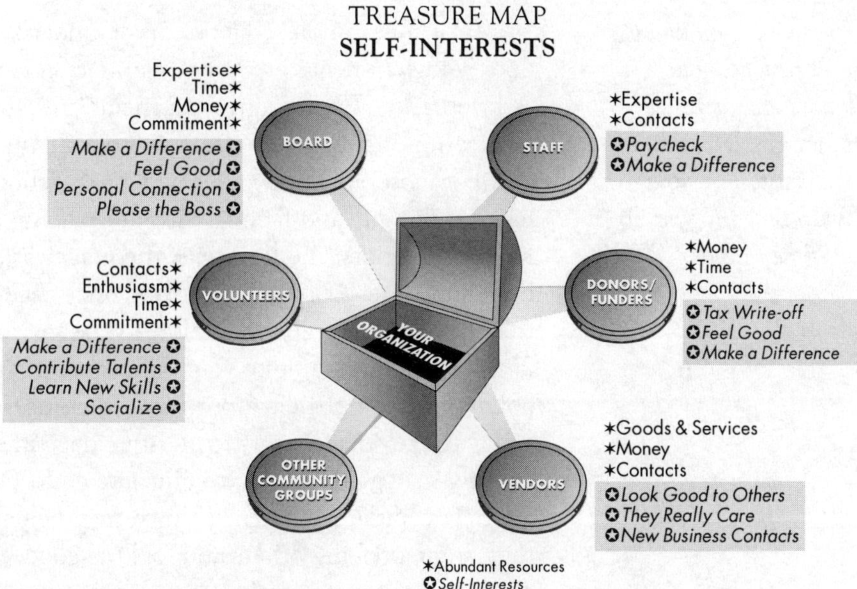

Self-Interest

Next, consider what would be the self-interest of the individuals in each group on your Treasure Map in coming to your Point of Entry Event. What would be the value or benefit for them in attending?

Let's pause a minute to talk about self-interest. Self-interest can be a good thing. It drives everything we do. For example, you have a definite self-interest in reading this book. Maybe that self-interest is finding new ideas, maybe it is pleasing the boss, or maybe it is because you wanted a break from your work. Self-interest is always there, and as a person who is interested in raising funds, you should think of it as a very useful resource.

Self-interest can range from the most negative and selfish motives all the way to the most noble and inspiring. Consider the full range of self-interest as you go back to your Treasure Map and list the potential benefits to each group.

The sooner you know what benefits your donors are interested in, the easier it will be to customize your fundraising program to meet their needs.

Take, for example, your donors or funders. What benefit does being connected to your organization have for them? Ask yourself, "What is in this for them?" Yes, they may want a tax write-off, but this is rarely the sole reason for making a gift. For most donors, a major benefit is feeling good about making the gift and feeling they are making a difference. For some donors, the benefit is the gratification of paying back someone for something they once received. Maybe they have a personal connection to the services you offer, or they feel that giving to your organization is an insurance policy protecting them from the bad thing your group is trying to prevent. Donors to an orphanage in a developing country may give, in part, to alleviate guilt. Donors to the big new capital campaign in town may benefit by feeling they are impressing others and looking good. Some donors give because they secretly hope to grease the skids of their child's or grandchild's application to your school or college.

Look at the self-interest of your volunteers. Why are they involved with you? Perhaps it is to make a difference, to contribute their talents, to learn new skills, to build their resume for their next job, to give back, to feel important, to keep busy, and on and on. What about your board? For some, their self-interest is to please a boss who "asked" them to serve on your board. For others, it is a personal connection, a way of giving back, or simply a feel-good thing.

Donor for donor, self-interest is a key driver of your self-sustaining individual giving program. The sooner you know what benefits your donors are interested in, the easier it will be to customize your fundraising program to meet their needs.

TREASURE MAP
FANTASY GROUPS

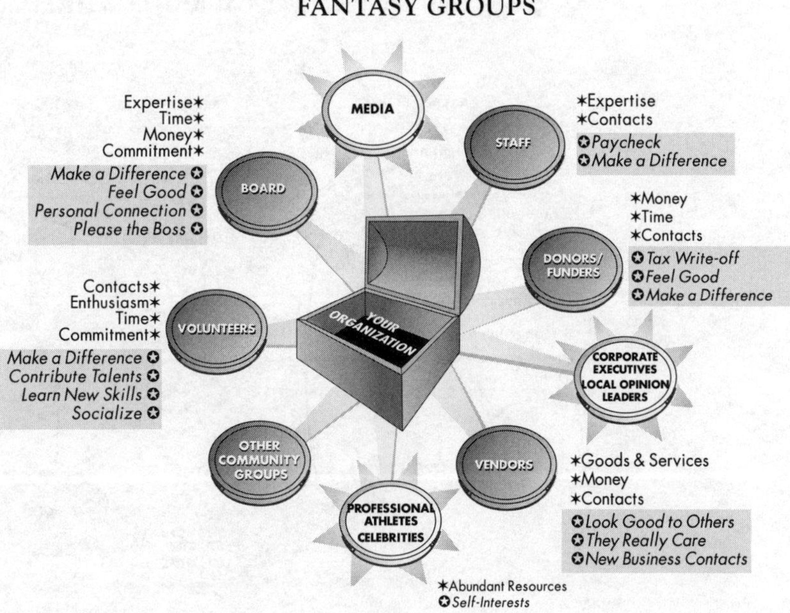

Dream Team

Looking back at your Treasure Map, add in some fantasy categories. Who is not yet on your map that you would love to have become associated with your organization? Whose involvement would leverage a whole world of support and credibility? Add those people to your Treasure Map, too. Some typical fantasy categories include celebrities, athletes, corporate executives, and media figures. For some organizations, having the support of a local opinion leader, a religious leader, or an expert on your issue could quickly leverage your story into the larger community.

Let yourself play with this one. This is why it is fun to make your Treasure Map with a group of people.

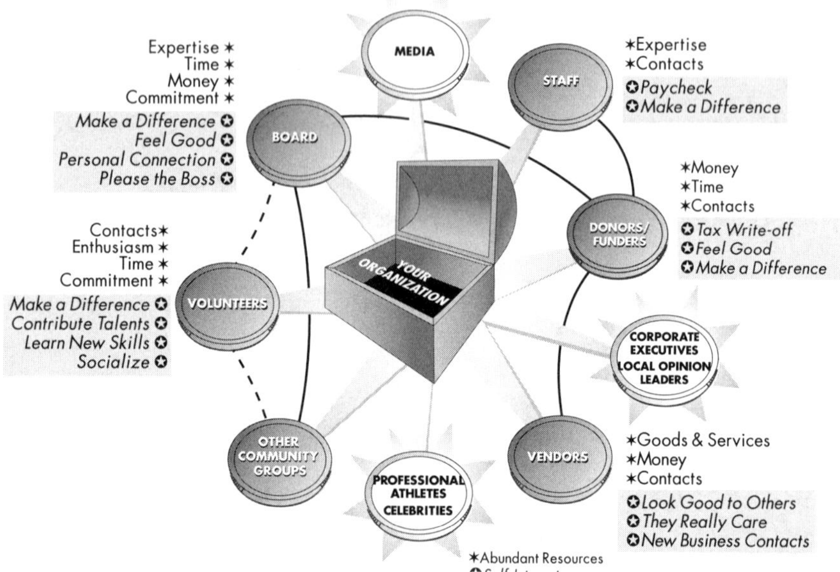

Connecting the Groups

It's time to draw connecting lines between those groups on your Treasure Map that are already talking to each other. You will see instantly how fast news can potentially travel. If a handful of people come to your sizzling Point of Entry Event, who else will they tell?

If your staff talks to your volunteers, draw a connecting line between those two groups. If your board and vendors talk only occasionally, you might draw a dotted line. For those groups who don't talk to each other at all, draw no connecting lines. Be sure to include your fantasy groups. Who on your organization's Treasure Map might already be talking with them? It is worth taking the time to go through this process one category at a time. It can spark many insights.

Before moving on, stand back from your Treasure Map and notice which groups have the most lines connecting them to other groups. There may be so many lines leading to or from one group that it looks like a traffic jam. What does that tell you? These groups are key to leveraging others. They could naturally invite the people in these other groups to attend your Point of Entry Events because they are often speaking to them anyway.

Adding to Your Gold-Standard List

As you look at the masterpiece your group has just created, you should be able to quickly identify a few more people who potentially meet the gold standard for Ambassadors. Add their names to your original short list, using the Ambassador chart below. Be careful not to allow wishful thinking to inflate your list with people who are not yet passionate about your work. Your total gold-standard Ambassador list at this point should have 10 to 20 names.

Next, fill in the "Who Will Invite Them to a Point of Entry Event" column in the Ambassador chart below. Also, be sure to fill in the "By When" column with the date by when each person will be invited to become an Ambassador. Otherwise, it may be easy to procrastinate.

Notice the last few lines of this chart, where you can list other people to invite as guests to Points of Entry. This is where you can add the names of all the other people from your Treasure Map who would have a natural reason to want to attend one of your Point of Entry Events but who are not yet close enough to the organization to become Ambassadors.

AMBASSADORS

Name of organization: ______________________ Today's date: ____________

Ambassadors	Who Will Invite Them to a Point of Entry Event	By When
1.		
2.		
3.		
4.		
5.		
6.		
7.		
8.		
9.		
10.		
11.		
12.		
13.		
14.		
15.		
16.		
17.		
18.		
19.		
20.		
Other People to Invite to Points of Entry		
1.		
2.		
3.		
4.		
5.		
6.		
7.		
8.		
9.		
10.		

Recruiting Ambassadors

Once your potential gold-standard Ambassadors have come to their first Point of Entry Event and given you their feedback about how to make it even better, you are ready to invite them to become an official Ambassador. Here are the Ambassador Volunteer Job Description and the Ambassador Invitation Script.

AMBASSADOR VOLUNTEER JOB DESCRIPTION

Ambassadors open doors for our organization in the community, introducing new people at our (Point of Entry Name).

Qualification:

Gold Standard: A passion for the mission of ________________.

Roles and Responsibilities:

1. Attends at least one Point of Entry each year.
2. Hosts or brings 10 to 15 guests to Point of Entry Events annually. This can be a Point of Entry in someone's home or office or at a regularly scheduled or private Point of Entry at the organization's offices.
3. Informs guests of what the Point of Entry will be about, and that they will receive one Follow-Up Call from the organization.
4. Attends the organization's Free Feel-Good Cultivation Events as desired.

Length of Service:

One year or until they complete their commitment to bring 10 people (usually takes approximately two to three months). Ambassador has the option to complete after one term, continue for another term, or move into another role on the team.

AMBASSADOR INVITATION SCRIPT

Ambassador Recruiter:

1. We are looking for people like you who are passionate about our work to become Ambassadors out in the community.
2. The Ambassador Program for (organization name) __________ is a special group of people who agree to bring 10 people to our __________ (Point of Entry) during the next year.
3. You could host a __________ (Point of Entry) at our office, your business, or in your home, and invite at least 10 friends to attend.
4. Or you could join your friends at one of our regularly scheduled, public ____________ (Point of Entry) throughout the year.
5. As an Ambassador you would be spreading the word about our work to (impact statement) ________.
6. Would you consider being an Ambassador for (organization name) ______________ for the next year?
7. Could I have (name of Ambassador Manager) _____________ give you a call in the next two days? He/she will walk you through the process to be a successful Ambassador.
8. Please have your calendar with you to schedule your Points of Entry.
9. Thank you again for agreeing to be an Ambassador.

Ambassador Manager:

- Thank you for agreeing to be an Ambassador for our organization.
- (Recruiter Name) ___________ asked me to support you in being a successful Ambassador.
- Would you like to host your own ____________ (Point of Entry) or bring friends to our regularly scheduled ___________ (Point of Entry)?
- Can we take a minute now to talk about who you would invite? Think about family, friends, etc. (Brainstorm a list of at least 15 names of people they can invite.)
- What dates and locations work best for you to begin? (Set dates for next two Points of Entry, so they will begin inviting their guests right away.)
- What is the best way to contact you, by phone or e-mail? (Set date for next contact.)

Thank you again for helping us spread the word about _______________ (organization name).

Notice that the Invitation Script above is divided into two sections: Ambassador Recruiter and Ambassador Manager.

The Ambassador Recruiter is the same person who makes the first Follow-Up Call after the Point of Entry Events. It is during this call that many guests will indicate an interest

The ideal scenario would be for each Ambassador to host one private Point of Entry Event at your location, with at least 10 guests in attendance, within three months of becoming an Ambassador.

in becoming more involved or inviting others to attend Points of Entry. When that happens, the follow-up caller becomes an Ambassador Recruiter, following steps 1-9 in the script above. They end the call by saying they will have the Ambassador Manager call the new Ambassador within the next day or two.

The Role of the Ambassador Manager

The Ambassador Manager becomes the Ambassador's ongoing contact person for the duration of their volunteer Ambassador agreement. The first call from the Ambassador Manager maps out the entire agreement, including:

When and where would the Ambassador like to have their Point of Entry Event?

Would the Ambassador prefer to host a private Point of Entry Event or invite guests to the organization's regularly scheduled public Points of Entry? The ideal scenario would be for each Ambassador to host one private Point of Entry Event at your location, with at least 10 guests in attendance, within three months of becoming an Ambassador. If the Ambassador is excited and has developed a guest list, there is no need to wait to have the event. Schedule their Point of Entry to take place as soon as possible. Choose the soonest date that works for everyone and make the event happen, capturing the initial momentum. Make sure the Ambassador knows this does not need to take a whole year.

It is not essential that the Ambassador have all 10 guests attend the same Point of Entry Event. They can invite two or three friends to each of your regularly scheduled public Points of Entry over the course of the next few months. Or they may prefer to host a private Point of Entry for 10 or more guests in their office, their home, their country club, or their church.

Be sure your Ambassador Manager takes time in that first phone call to help the new Ambassador brainstorm a full Personal Treasure Map…

Although the easiest location for your staff will no doubt be in the organization's office, where your team will already have practiced and refined your program, we will talk more about taking your Point of Entry Events on the road, which we call a Point of Entry in a Box, in Chapter 16.

Who will the Ambassador invite to attend?

Be sure your Ambassador Manager takes time in that first phone call to help the new Ambassador brainstorm a full Personal Treasure Map, identifying specific social or professional groups, book clubs, etc., that the person belongs to. Do not assume they will do this without you.

Have them walk through the same steps as the Treasure Map you made for your organization, starting by putting themselves in the center circle, adding the groups they naturally come in contact with, what each group has in abundance, the benefits for the groups in coming to a Point of Entry Event for your organization, their fantasy groups, and the lines connecting those who know each other. Give them enough time to go through all the steps. They probably will be surprised by all the treasure they have.

Then, ask them to make a list of 10 to 20 individuals from the various categories on their Treasure Map who they would feel comfortable inviting to a Point of Entry Event. It's often easiest for people to start off by inviting the people closest to them: friends and family. Beyond that, is there a ready-made group they are part of? Does that group have a standing meeting time? Would that be a group that might have an interest in coming to your Point of Entry Event?

How will the Ambassador and Ambassador Manager stay in regular contact with each other?

Before you end your initial call with your new Ambassador, ask the all-important question: what is the best way to stay in touch with you? Arrange a formal or informal frequency and method of contact, such as a phone call every other week, a weekly e-mail, or an in-person meeting once a month.

You do not want Ambassadors feeling burdened by having to dig deeper through their finite list of contacts to help you each year.

Final Thoughts on Building Your Ambassador Program

Many groups set a goal of having two Points of Entry per month for their first year of implementing the Benevon Model. One of those events each month will be hosted by an Ambassador who invites their own circle of friends, family, or business associates. The second Point of Entry Event each month will be hosted by your organization. Your staff, board, and volunteers may invite people you identified in the Treasure Map exercise, even if they do not choose to become official Ambassadors. Regardless of who invites the guests, each Point of Entry Event should be powerful enough to generate one new Ambassador in the follow-up process.

As for how to organize your Ambassadors into a group, there is no required format. Some groups make their Ambassador program very formal, with ribbons and badges, social events and celebrations. Others keep it very low-key, talking one-on-one with their Ambassadors to schedule their Points of Entry.

In terms of length of service, people generally volunteer as Ambassadors for one year, two years at most. Your goal and theirs should be to have each of their Point of Entry Events generate one new Ambassador, who in turn hosts 10 guests at a Point of Entry over the next year. You do not want Ambassadors feeling burdened by having to dig deeper through their finite list of contacts to help you each year.

Plan each Ambassador's succession right from the start. Some Ambassadors have large networks and may invite 50 guests the first year, 30 the next and so on. But eventually they will run out of people who will say yes when invited

We tell our groups that passion is the glue that holds the whole model together.

to a Point of Entry Event. At that point or sooner, consider inviting them to take on another role in your organization, perhaps as a member of your Sustainable Funding Team or your board. Certainly a person who spreads the word and follows through by having many guests is a person of interest for future involvement with your organization.

We tell our groups that passion is the glue that holds the whole model together. You and your team must be passionate about the work of the organization. Your Ambassadors must be extremely passionate about your work. Your Point of Entry Event must convey that deep passion and really connect with the guests. In that way, those guests for whom your organization's mission really is their life's work or their natural calling will be inspired to join you by becoming Ambassadors and inviting others to the very same type of event that just inspired them: your Point of Entry Event.

Now that you have learned how to launch and manage your Ambassador Program, let's turn to a second key method for ensuring a steady stream of Point of Entry Guests, the Know-Thy-Donor Program.

Know-Thy-Donor

The second method for filling your Points of Entry is what we call a Know-Thy-Donor or Know-Thy-Volunteer Program.

As you no doubt saw when you made your organization's Treasure Map, you have a category on your Treasure Map called donors. Around that category you were able to draw subcategories for donors who have given through various methods: direct-mail donors, walkathon donors, and auction donors, for instance. In the volunteer categories it is the same: you can create subcategories by looking at program volunteers such as tutors, Meals-on-Wheels delivery volunteers, or fundraising volunteers who help

While we find that most groups we work with have many lists and categories for donors, volunteers, and members, they do not know many of those people well.

with events and mailings. Some groups also have members and subgroups of members, for example museum members or hiking club members.

While we find that most groups we work with have many lists and categories for donors, volunteers, and members, they do not know many of those people well. These lists are a perfect source of potential Point of Entry guests and people to engage in the entire process. We call this a Know-Thy-Donor Program and here is how it works.

Stratify Your Donors by Gift Level

Start your Know-Thy-Donor Program by getting your organization's real baseline numbers. How many individual donors have given to you in the last two years? What is each donor's total gift for each of those years? Notice how quickly those $25-a-month checks add up, all from one loyal donor.

Now, classify the donors you have. How many give you, annually:

- $1,000 and above?
- $500 to $999?

Don't be surprised to find some donors who give more than $10,000 a year without a personal contact from you.

What are they telling you with this gift? For whatever reason, they are believers in your mission. They may have only a superficial understanding of the work of your organization, yet they give. Perhaps they had a family member with the disease you are working to eradicate. Maybe their mother or father received services from your organization many years ago.

If you are working to build a self-sustaining individual giving program that is based on one-on-one personal relationships, knowing more about each donor would be a great help. And there is only one way to find out—ask them!

If you accomplish nothing else on this call, be sure they know how much you appreciate them.

Once you've analyzed the stratification of your existing donors, choose the cutoff level for your first round of calls. Let's say you decide to call all donors who give $500 or more a year and that you have 100 of them.

Conduct a High-Level Thank-a-Thon

The next step in your Know-Thy-Donor program is to enlist the support of a small group of your most passionate supporters—who also like talking on the telephone. It may be a mixed group of board, staff, and volunteers.

Before you give them the list of donors to be called and a recommended script, it is wise for the most senior development staff person or volunteer to make the first 10 of these calls personally. That way you will get consistent feedback, all screened through the eyes and ears of the same caller. Based on what you learn in the first 10 calls, you can then design a broader telephone survey that can be used by your team of callers.

When you are ready to put together a group of board and staff to phone these current donors personally, you can call it a thank-a-thon.

Once again, imagine yourself as one of those loyal donors to your favorite organization. You have been giving faithfully for years, sending in checks in response to mail or phone appeals annually, quarterly, or monthly. Yet no one has ever called you to say thank you or to acknowledge your gift in person. It is a wonder you keep giving.

How should you start the calls? Yes, with a gracious and humble thank you. The main purpose of the call is to thank and appreciate the donor for their loyal support (and their recent gift if your timing is right). If you accomplish nothing else on this call, be sure they know how much you appreciate them. Beyond that, you want to learn as much as you can about their reasons for supporting your organization.

Here is a suggested outline for the call:

Hello, Ms. _________. My name is ____________. I'm on the board of ______________. You've been a loyal supporter for several/many years, and we're calling to thank you. (Pause for response.) We are trying to gather input about what we could be doing better. Would you have a few minutes now for me to ask for your thoughts and advice?

Ask Treasure Map Interview Questions

Then, slowly, ask three or four of the open-ended Treasure Map Interview questions listed here, noting the donor's answers along the way. The questions below are typical, but you should do your own work to come up with a list of questions that reflect what your organization wants to know.

1. What do you already know about our organization?
2. What images come to mind when you think of us?
3. How did you come to know about us or become involved with us?
4. What do you like about being a friend/supporter of our organization?
5. Where or how do you think we're really missing the boat?
6. What advice do you have for us?
7. What cues might we have missed from you?
8. How better could we be telling our story?
9. What could we be doing to involve more people?

Invite Them to a Point of Entry Event

Each call should end with an invitation to attend a Point of Entry or, if they are already a donor, a Point of Re-Entry (Free Feel-Good Cultivation Event) and to bring others if they would like. If they agree to attend, follow up with a

Imagine a donor who hears from someone at their favorite nonprofit organization three or four times a year—including invitations to a particular Free Feel-Good Cultivation Event focusing on their specific program area of interest.

confirmation card and a reconfirmation call the day before. Offer to provide them with transportation if necessary.

Your thank-a-thon calling team can do the phoning in a group one afternoon or evening. Or they can make their calls on their own from their home or workplace. Be sure their notes are put into your database tracking system. If, for example, five callers each spoke with 10 people, you would have enough feedback to customize the next phase of the program.

I have seen board members get so excited about this that they recommend a cultivation program pairing a volunteer or staff member with each donor above a certain dollar amount for two years. Imagine a donor who hears from someone at their favorite nonprofit organization three or four times a year—including invitations to a particular Free Feel-Good Cultivation Event focusing on their specific program area of interest. When it is time for making an annual gift next year, they will be hard-pressed to say no to a request for a larger gift. They may even feel connected enough to make a multiple-year pledge when asked, especially if it will be doubled by a Leadership or Challenge Gift.

Know-Thy-Volunteer/Member

This same stratifying, calling, interviewing, and inviting strategy can be implemented with your volunteers and your members. Just be sure the callers are people from that same group. For example, have your most passionate and well-respected volunteer tutors call your other volunteer tutors. That way they can address their concerns. A volunteer to a literacy center might say, "As a volunteer tutor, I never paid much attention to the other activities going on at the literacy center. I just came in once a week, met with my student for two hours, and left feeling very satisfied that I had

That type of warm and personal invitation from a colleague tells your volunteers that you value them.

made a contribution. Once I attended the Literacy Center's ______________ (Point of Entry Event), all of my work as a volunteer came into focus. I saw the larger picture and where we fit in. I was so moved by the wonderful things being done here. I offered to call the other tutors to thank you for giving your time and to invite you to a special _______ (Point of Entry Event) just for the volunteer tutors. We picked a time we thought would be convenient for the majority of us, since most of us are here on Thursday afternoons anyway. I really hope you can join us for an hour. I think it will inspire you and, hopefully, open your eyes, like it did mine."

Then the caller gives the details of the Point of Entry Event and follows up if needed to see if the guest will attend. That type of warm and personal invitation from a colleague tells your volunteers that you value them.

Make these Point of Entry Events special. Have a brief social time at the start, with some light snacks and soft drinks. You can start by having each tutor say how long they've been volunteering and their favorite thing about the job they do. Introduce the person who will be making the Follow-Up Calls and be sure this person has a speaking role during the Point of Entry Event. Make sure the Visionary Leader—your executive director or CEO—genuinely acknowledges these valuable volunteers. Then do your standard Point of Entry Event, showcasing all three of your bucket areas, so the volunteers learn the other aspects of your work. Share the myths, the facts, the stories, and the needs. End with a testimonial from a student or parent.

When your staff member makes the Follow-Up Calls, don't be surprised by the number of guests who will say, "I had no idea!" Many of these same volunteers will want to become Ambassadors. After all, who better to become an Ambassador than a gold-standard volunteer?

CHAPTER 7

STEP FOUR: DETERMINING HOW MUCH IS ENOUGH

Once you have secured the support of your board for implementing the Benevon Model, assembled your team, and clarified your game plan for engaging your community, the next step is to get very specific about your organization's measurable definition of sustainable funding.

We say that attaining sustainable funding requires each nonprofit organization to clarify its specific metrics, timeline, and plan for reaching the goal. Otherwise it will never happen.

To inspire each team to think big, we challenge them to imagine what life would be like at their organization if worrying about funding were no longer an issue. What if the basic day-to-day financial needs were handled and your organization could move onto fulfilling the next level of your mission—developing the programs you know would make a difference, staffing the departments that leverage the greatest results in the community, undergirding your infrastructure to sustain your operations going forward? How would that change the self-image of your organization, the quality of the work, and the outcomes?

What would have to have happened to make that possible? How much money would be in the bank and by when? How many months of operating reserves would it take for your organization to feel secure: three months, one year, two years? How many individual donors would you have? Would you want to have a big endowment?

Even with a generous endowment, there was still plenty of fundraising and other work to be done to fulfill the school's larger mission.

At the school where I began to develop the Benevon Model, our definition of sustainable funding ultimately included an endowment fund that was large enough to generate in interest enough money to cover the annual operational gap that we struggled to raise each year. This does not mean, however, that after we had funded our endowment, the school no longer needed to raise funds. On the contrary, they worked as hard as ever to raise more funds and to engage the community in their work.

Like your organization's mission, the mission of the school was broader than just educating its current students. They wanted to dispel myths, build bridges in the community, educate more students, and support their families. Having an endowment that covered much of the annual financial operating gap meant the administrators were not waking up in the middle of the night worrying about closing the school's doors. Even with a generous endowment, there was still plenty of fundraising and other work to be done to fulfill the school's larger mission.

Quantifying Your Legacy

Each group uses different metrics to track their progress in fulfilling their objectives. Some define sustainability as an endowment large enough to throw off in earnings enough money to cover their annual operating shortfall or gap. Their ultimate metric might be to have a $20 million endowment that will generate $1 million a year in income.

Other groups define sustainability as a reserve fund or pot of money set aside that they can get their hands on when they need it. They may decide, for example, that if they had a reserve fund large enough to cover one year's operations, they could manage the uncertainties of their multiple funding sources year by year. That one year's reserve fund becomes their metric.

Far and away, the number-one benefit our groups report from implementing the Benevon Model is that they are no longer the "best-kept secret" in town.

Some groups define sustainability as having a higher percentage of their revenue coming from individual donors. Instead of having 95% of their revenue coming from government grants, 4% from corporations and foundations, and 1% from individuals, their metric may be to increase the 1% from individual giving to 5%.

Still other groups define sustainability as a percentage increase in the number of individual donors they now have, for example, increasing their current number of 200 major donors by 100% to 400 major donors. Of course, each group would define "major" donor for itself.

Another metric might be increasing the raw number of individual donors by a certain amount, for example, adding 100 new major donors per year, or reaching a total of 500 donors. Groups might put specific conditions on these goals, such as requiring that each donor has an ongoing open pledge to contribute at least $1,000 a year for each of the next five years. Their metric is the number of new donors at these levels.

In addition to establishing hard financial and donor metrics, we encourage each group to quantify their goals for softer intangibles like broader community awareness, more people requesting to become board members or volunteers, favorable media coverage, and more support from foundations and businesses. For many groups, these softer benefits are more valuable than the money raised.

Far and away, the number-one benefit our groups report from implementing the Benevon Model is that they are no longer the "best-kept secret" in town. People know them now. One behavioral health organization we work with is located in a rural community with a population of only 2,500 people. Yet people in the town did not know what was really going on inside their building. By the end of their first year using the model, all that had changed. They now had business support, favorable media coverage, and many passionate

The legacy you want to leave needs to be crystal clear before you begin to implement the systematic approach provided by the Benevon Model.

advocates championing their work at public meetings and the state legislature at budget time. Those results are hard to quantify.

We also understand that each organization's metrics for attaining sustainable funding may change over time. As they achieve one goal, such as having a reserve fund of a specific amount, they may decide next to embark on a capital campaign or build an endowment, goals which may have been unthinkable until now.

Here are the specific questions to guide this important discussion with your group:

1. How will we quantify our legacy of sustainable funding for this organization?
   a. Short-term goals for the next five years?
   b. Long-term goals for the next 10 to 15 years?
   Be sure to include in these goals specific metrics, for example:
   - $25 million endowment
   - Reserve fund of one year's operating expenses
   - 20% increase in individual donors
   - Diversifying funding sources by increasing funding from individual donors by 20%
2. What would be the impact of attaining this legacy?
   a. On the people we serve?
   b. On our community?

The legacy you want to leave needs to be crystal clear before you begin to implement the systematic approach provided by the Benevon Model. Take the time you need to quantify—and get excited about—what sustainable funding would look like for your organization. You will need it to inspire your group as you embark on the work ahead!

Let's move on to designing your Multiple-Year Giving Society, which is key to the process of attaining sustainable funding in the Benevon Model.

CHAPTER 8

STEP FIVE: DESIGNING YOUR MULTIPLE-YEAR GIVING SOCIETY

As you get ready to launch the Benevon Model, you will also need to design and name your new Multiple-Year Giving Society. This is the giving club for donors making pledges of $1,000 or more per year for a minimum of five years. While many of your new donors may choose to give less than $1,000 for five years, our model requires a minimum pledge of $1,000 a year for five years in order to qualify as a member of your Multiple-Year Giving Society.

Why Multiple-Year Pledges?

Multiple-year pledges have traditionally been used as a payment tool for large gifts for unrestricted use, capital needs, or endowment, allowing donors the flexibility to spread their gift over multiple tax years, for example. But multiple-year pledges for an annual gift have traditionally been regarded as a bad idea. Generally these annual gifts were thought to be too small, or that the pledge payoff rate for them would be poor, or that the donor would be reluctant to increase their annual gift each year.

That line of thinking would seem to make sense, however, we have seen quite the opposite. We have found that donors are willing and able to make larger pledges for unrestricted operational funding and to pay off those pledges faithfully over time.

They know they don't have to make a five-year pledge to your organization—they want to!

I believe this is because these donors have read the pledge form carefully (page 212) and have chosen, quite deliberately, to make these larger multiple-year gifts. They see that they also have the "fill-in-the-blank" option to give whatever amount they would like for as many years as they would like.

They could make a gift of, say, $1,000 a year for one year at a time. That is a significant gift. Your organization would no doubt thank them, cultivate them, and odds are they would continue to give at that level or higher.

Therefore donors who choose to join the Multiple-Year Giving Society, making pledges of at least $1,000 a year for five years, are sending you a clear message.

They know they don't have to make a five-year pledge to your organization—they want to!

That is a critical amount of permission from a donor. It is as if that donor is saying to your organization, "That mission of yours, that work you're doing, that issue you're working to solve in the world, that's my work too. It doesn't mean I will necessarily give you all the money you ever ask for, it just means that I'm with you on the mission. Count me in, come ask for my advice, include me as part of your organization's family."

Why is this permission so essential? Because it tells you where to focus your donor cultivation efforts. These new Multiple-Year Giving Society donors should be treated as your organization's new best friends. If they are able to give such significant gifts at your Free One-Hour Ask Event, what else might be possible if you were able to get to know them better and involve them in whatever way they prefer in the life of your organization? These are the people who become your new Ambassadors, formally or informally opening doors, sharing the message about your mission, and inviting others to get to know you.

In other words, the purpose of the multiple-year pledge is not for the organization. As wonderful as you will feel

The purpose of the multiple-year pledge is for the donor.

waking up on January 1 of your second year of using the Benevon Model, when you realize you have a large number of pledges to be paid in the coming year, and as happy as you will be to show the bank or the board all the pledges you have coming in, that is not the real purpose of securing multiple-year pledges. The purpose of the multiple-year pledge is for the donor.

Why Five Years?

Many groups that have been implementing the Benevon Model on their own tell us they have been reluctant to ask for five-year pledges. Their alternative seems to be asking for three-year pledges. *If you are committed to getting it right, this issue is non-negotiable*. In our testing and tracking, we have found that three-year pledges are not nearly as effective. Three years go by quickly. Many groups have not gotten to know their donors at all in those three years, ensuring a low pledge-payoff rate and a very poor pledge-renewal rate. Three years is not enough time for the model to take hold in your organization.

Some groups that come to our program after implementing the Benevon Model on their own tell us that they chose three-year pledges for fear of scaring off donors by asking for five-year pledges right from the start. We try to reassure them by reminding them that launching the five-year Multiple-Year Giving Society in no way precludes single-year giving. The fill-in-the-blank box on the pledge card will engender many one-year gifts from those more comfortable with year-by-year gifts.

If you already have a strong base of year-by-year donors, as part of your Know-Thy-Donor Program you will be inviting them to special Points of Entry for existing donors and, eventually, inviting them to become part of your new Multiple-Year Giving Society, either one-on-one or at your

By having these three specific Units of Service, people knew what we needed.

Ask Event. If they decline this invitation, their names will still be listed in your annual report using the same categories you have used in the past.

Units of Service

Your Units of Service are the three giving levels within your Multiple-Year Giving Society. They are the incremental dollar amounts of unrestricted funding you will be asking for. You must have three (and only three) levels.

You may be wondering why you would even need specific giving levels. After all, if your donors have been well cultivated and they come to your inspiring Ask Event, wouldn't it seem obvious to them what you want them to do? Actually, no.

For example, at our school's first Ask Event, when it was time for the Pitch Person to ask for money, imagine if instead of asking for the three specific giving levels, he had said, "Please give generously. Give from the bottom of your hearts."

What does that mean? In this day and age, people would not know the proper thing to do in that situation. Those with the capacity to make a big gift might be nervous about giving too much and standing out. And those with less giving capacity may feel self-conscious about giving too little; they may feel their small gift is not significant enough to matter.

By having these three specific Units of Service, people knew what we needed. Many people did the math. They realized that $1,000 a year is $83 a month and many people said, "Yes, I can do that, I believe that much in what I just saw. Sign me up!"

I believe that had we not had our three Units of Service and a clear script for our Pitch Person to follow when inviting people to join the Multiple-Year Giving Society, our first event would have raised significantly less money.

Note that the lowest level in both options is $1,000 a year for five years.

Choosing Your Giving Levels

There are two (and only two) options for these levels, which are determined based on past giving history in your organization. Once you establish your three levels, they never change:

- Option 1: $1,000, $5,000, and $10,000 a year for five years
- Option 2: $1,000, $10,000, and $25,000 a year for five years

Note that the lowest level in both options is $1,000 a year for five years. A donor who gives anything over that amount—and pledges to continue to give that amount for five years—is considered to be a member of your Multiple-Year Giving Society, even if they do not give at exactly one of your three giving levels. For example, a donor who pledges to give $2,500 a year for five years would definitely be a member of your giving society.

To determine which of the two giving level options to use, answer this question: in the past two years, has your organization received a gift from an individual donor of $10,000 or higher? If not, you must use the three giving levels in Option 1 above. If so, then your three giving levels must be the higher levels in Option 2 above.

Many self-implementing groups add a fourth or fifth giving level, further complicating their giving society, mostly out of fear that donors will not give to them at the higher levels for five years.

To repeat: if you are committed to getting it right, you may not have more than three giving levels.

Why $1,000 as the Lowest Level?

Many of these same groups are reluctant to ask for $1,000 a year for five years as their lowest giving level to entitle a donor to be in the giving society, preferring a lower entry level like $500. They feel that asking for $1,000 a year for

Again, if you are committed to getting it right, stick with five-year pledges with your lowest giving level at $1,000 a year.

five years is much too large a gift for the people in their community who will be coming to their Ask Event. We have tested these lower levels and have found, again, that groups willing to follow our recommendation and start at $1,000 a year for five years are pleasantly surprised by the number of people who opt in at that level. Those wishing to give less certainly will take the opportunity to use the fill-in-the-blank box on the pledge card.

Non-Negotiable

These issues are absolutely "non-negotiable" with the groups we train and coach in our Benevon programs. Again, if you are committed to getting it right, stick with five-year pledges with your lowest giving level at $1,000 a year.

Designing Your Giving Society and Units of Service

Take some time to come up with a strong overall name for your Multiple-Year Giving Society since it will be with your organization for years. Look to the name of your Point of Entry Event and your three buckets or areas of impact, since you will want your three giving levels to be named similarly. For example, the three giving levels for a family service organization might be: Supporting Individuals, Strengthening Families, and Building Communities, and they might name their Multiple-Year Giving Society the Preserving Families Society.

A faith-based hospital might name their levels: Gift of Hope, Gift of Health, and Gift of Healing and call their society the St. James Society.

A land use group's three levels might be: Protect, Restore, and Steward, and they might call their society the Preservation Society.

...these levels represent arbitrary chunks of needed, unrestricted operating funds.

For an advocacy group, the three levels in their Circle of Change Society might be: Visionary, Peacemaker, and Changemaker.

The main thing to keep in mind as you design your Units of Service is that you will be making it clear to your donors that these levels represent arbitrary chunks of needed, unrestricted operating funds. They will be giving at these levels because they believe in your overall mission. They trust you to get the job done. If they have questions about your use of funds, they can always review your organization's public financial information.

Recognizing Multiple-Year Giving Society Donors in Your Annual Report

Be sure to list your Multiple-Year Giving Society members prominently as a separate category in your annual report, right above your annual givers. Use a headline that calls attention to the fact that these people have agreed to give at these levels for five years or longer.

Do Not Change Levels

Once you have designed your units, do not change them. Although you will not be using these larger levels for your traditional direct mail appeals, the pledge form you design for your Ask Event will be the same pledge form you use in all of your one-on-one major gift solicitations. As you become comfortable with the levels you have designed, you will find it easy to make all of your Asks at one of these levels.

As an example of the power of having a Multiple-Year Giving Society, I often tell the story about asking for a contribution from the owner of a large, privately held corporation. This man had attended a Point of Entry Event and had been well followed-up and cultivated. He was definitely ready to

If you have followed the Benevon Model, not skipped over any of the steps, and have your Units of Service well thought out, an Ask of a well-cultivated donor can be that simple.

be asked. Because of his heavy travel schedule, I had been unable to connect with him by phone to even schedule a time we could get together to discuss his gift.

A month or so later, I happened to nearly bump into this man as he was walking out of an elevator in the lobby of an office building. Our 20-second conversation went something like this:

"Hi, Terry, how are you? I know I owe you a call."

"Yes, that's okay. You know why I was calling."

"Yep, I do. What's everybody giving?"

"$25,000 a year for five years to 'Sponsor a Classroom' of kids."

"That sounds great. Sign us up!"

If you have followed the Benevon Model, not skipped over any of the steps, and have your Units of Service well thought out, an Ask of a well-cultivated donor can be that simple. In the case of this man, after each Ask, he attended more of our "missionized" high-end donor Free Feel-Good Cultivation Events. With close personal follow-up over time, he has become a major donor to the organization's capital and endowment campaigns, while continuing to give a $25,000 gift annually as part of his ongoing five-year pledge to the Multiple-Year Giving Society.

CHAPTER 9

STEP SIX: RESULTS YOU CAN MEASURE—HAVING A TRACKING SYSTEM THAT WORKS

Your organization's donor database is the collective institutional memory of the entire cultivation process. Long after your staff, board, and volunteers have moved on, your database will live on as the one reliable archive chronicling each donor's relationship with your organization.

Use your database to track Point of Entry guests, information gathered from each question in the Follow-Up Call, cultivation contacts, volunteer involvement, Ambassador activity, Ask Event Table Captains, gifts and pledges, ongoing major gifts cultivation, and one-on-one Asks. Rather than regard the database as a burden or annoyance or something to be "managed" by someone who is peripheral to the process, I have always thought of my database as the full-time equivalent of a super-smart staff member or member of my team. I recommend you design it to be something that you and each team member can rely on as their personal memory bank, diary, or journal. In other words, consider that your tracking system could be something you love.

Furthermore, if it is properly secured, easy to use, readily accessible to everyone on your team, and linked to a calendar function, it can become an easy and natural way to

Your database is a huge part of your legacy. Even after your group has successfully achieved all of your initial financial goals, you will need that collective repository for future generations.

communicate updates on donor contacts, manage the next contacts for each donor, and manage your overall cultivation calendar as well.

I clearly recall, way back in 1992, purchasing the first database program for our school with my own money. I knew then that if I was going to be successful as the sole staff member working on fundraising, a great database would be essential. Most of my days were spent sitting at a little desk in front of my computer screen with my headset on, reconfirming Point of Entry guests, making Follow-Up Calls, making phone calls to supporters and donors, and tracking every single conversation in our database. Years after I left the school, subsequent development directors thanked me for setting up that database and for the quality and detail of my notes, which taught them the importance of entering such critical information.

Your database is a huge part of your legacy. Even after your group has successfully achieved all of your initial financial goals, you will need that collective repository for future generations.

Back then, in the early 1990s, having a computer database of any type was considered very progressive. I was pretty much working alone, so one desktop computer and one software package made sense. Fast-forward to today, and I would certainly recommend something Web-based that everyone on your team can use. It's ideal to have a database that functions more like a private Web site for your team, where everyone can enter their notes, check on the status of various donor cultivation plans, and assign next steps after every single contact to ensure that no donor is left to fall between the cracks. Of course, you will be able to password-protect certain fields, such as the gift history, if desired.

Several years ago, we set out to find such software that we could customize for the Benevon Model and recommend to our groups. We chose eTapestry, a Blackbaud company, to partner with Benevon to design Next Step, an inexpensive, Web-based, private-label Benevon version of their basic product. Here is a listing of what that Web-based software allows you to track. Whether you choose to use our product or another one, if you are serious about implementing the model, your donor relationship software needs to meet all of the following requirements.

Tracking System Requirements

- Tracks relationships and contacts over time, not just basic contact information and gift history
- Easy to use by everyone on your team
- Interfaces with your Web site, so that Web site information is captured directly into the database
- Delivers and stores individual and mass e-mail
- Provides a log of contacts
- Integrates with your calendar and tickler system, so that all notes have dates and action items that link to the appropriate date in your daily planner
- Tracks relationships between people
- Tracks which events people attended (when invited and by whom)
- Tracks which mailings/contacts people responded to
- Tracks Follow-Up Call dates, messages left, and what was said on the call
- The Follow-Up Call form is included in the database and answers to the five questions can be filled in there

To summarize, your tracking system should be the one solid, reliable repository for the chronology of every contact with each donor, potential donor, and volunteer. That is the only way everyone who has access to your database will come to count on this as the sole source for up-to-the-minute information on each donor.

CHAPTER 10

STEP SEVEN: DESIGNING YOUR CLASSIC POINT OF ENTRY EVENT

Imagine having a one-hour get-acquainted event about your organization that was so powerful that every single guest left saying, "What a remarkable organization! I had no idea you did all of that." What if you didn't have to carefully select the "right" guests based on their giving capacity or stature in the community, but rather you could invite anyone and everyone to attend? Then, when you called each guest to follow up, every single person told you how inspired they were by your work? Even if the majority of the guests chose not to become more involved, they would have been touched enough by your work that they would naturally tell others.

That's the *point* of the Point of Entry Event!

The Point of Entry Event is the centerpiece and engine of the Benevon Model for Sustainable Funding. We call it a "tour of your mission." Your goal should be to test and refine this event over time, tweaking program elements, stories, and tour stops until your one-hour Point of Entry is reliably and consistently inspiring people and moving them to tears. That's how good this event needs to be.

The truest test of the impact of your Point of Entry Event will be whether the guests invite others to attend future Points of Entry. Friends won't invite their friends to something that's just mediocre or "nice." It has truly got to be life-changing so that guests will be inspired to tell others about your organization and encourage them to attend.

That tour of your programs or facilities is not what we mean by a Point of Entry Event.

Most groups we work with already have some version of a tour they can dust off and conduct if someone important comes to visit. Perhaps it is an orientation tour to attract new students to a college or private school, a summer camp visiting day for parents, a volunteer recruitment event, or a hands-on work day. If a funder were to call you and say they were considering giving your organization $25,000 but they wanted to come and visit you first, you would definitely figure out something to show them!

Most likely, you would start with a meeting in the conference room or the executive director's office and then take them on a tour of your programs and facilities. You would try to dazzle them with as many facts and statistics as possible. You would probably, unwittingly, use more jargon than they would understand and tell few powerful stories, or tell your stories too superficially, because, ironically, the life-changing impact of your organization's work may have become a bit second nature to you. Your guests could easily be left over-informed and underwhelmed. Most critically, they would not know specifically what you needed. While they would know that you are passionate about your work, they wouldn't be able to clearly convey much about your work to a friend. They would be reluctant to invite anyone to come back and take a similar tour.

That tour of your programs or facilities is not what we mean by a Point of Entry Event.

A Point of Entry Event is a tightly choreographed, seemingly casual one-hour *tour of your mission*. In 60 short minutes, people should be moved to tears at least three times. They will have learned several startling, myth-buster facts and they will understand clearly your specific needs. Guests should leave your Point of Entry Event so inspired they will immediately be on their cell phones calling and texting their friends and family, telling them, "You've got to see what I just saw!" If your Point of Entry Event is that

We had repeatedly tested and arrived at the fewest number of guest speakers—teachers, board members, volunteers—we needed to conduct the Point of Entry.

good, the ripple effect will take hold and your inspired guests will be spreading the word about your work very naturally, friend to friend. At least one guest from each Point of Entry Event will become an Ambassador for your organization, an official messenger who invites at least 10 people to Point of Entry Events in the next few months, thereby assuring an ongoing steady stream of guests who in turn will spread the word further and invite others.

At our school in Seattle where the Benevon Model was started, we had nearly 1,100 people attend our Point of Entry Events in the first five months. Each guest had been invited word-of-mouth, friend-to-friend! We certainly were not putting ads in the newspapers or offering incentive prizes to our volunteers or board members to pressure their friends to attend. It was because, after refining and tweaking the Point of Entry program time after time, based on the honest and generous feedback we heard in our Follow-Up Calls from our Point of Entry guests, we were able to boil our message down to its very essence.

We knew exactly which time of day worked best, which classrooms to stop at during our tour and in what sequence, and which stories to tell. We had repeatedly tested and arrived at the fewest number of guest speakers—teachers, board members, volunteers—we needed to conduct the Point of Entry. We had figured out just how much of our principal's valuable time we needed for the Point of Entry to have the full impact.

It took time and hard work and an enormous commitment on the part of our board, our teachers, and the school administration to stick with the Point of Entry process for those first nine months leading up to our first Ask Event. At that first Ask Event, over 80% of the guests had attended one of these Point of Entry Events, and in many cases had invited many others to attend them as well. That is the only reason our first Free One-Hour Ask Event raised nearly $1.5

The first place to look is to your organization's mission statement. Often you'll find the buckets right there.

million. It correlated directly with the percentage of ripened fruit and the diligent, rigorous work that had been done getting people to attend the Points of Entry, following up and engaging people one by one.

Choosing Your Buckets

Before we walk through each step of the Point of Entry agenda, we need to tackle the biggest challenge: how to describe the impact of the multitude of programs and services your organization offers in a one-hour Point of Entry Event.

To do this, you will need to craft your succinct Mission Message, which begins by organizing all that you do into three areas of impact, or "buckets."

Pretend that you have three large empty buckets in front of you. Now try to divide all your programs into one of the three buckets. How would you name the buckets so that every program is included?

The first place to look is to your organization's mission statement. Often you'll find the buckets right there. For example, the mission statement of the American Red Cross includes the words, "help people prevent, prepare for, and respond to emergencies." Everything the Red Cross does can come under one of those three buckets or areas of impact: prevent, prepare, respond.

Another way to choose your buckets is from the "user's" experience. A potential client arriving at the door of a large nonprofit serving adults with disabilities, we'll call it the Abilities in Action Center, might be looking for assistance with jobs, housing, and transportation. Everything Abilities in Action does can be sorted into one of those three buckets. Another way to say that might be: self-sufficiency, shelter, and mobility. Or you can add a verb in front of each bucket and have: promoting self-sufficiency, securing shelter, and ensuring mobility.

As you look to assign each of your programs to a bucket, don't worry if some of your programs span all three buckets.

What are some other examples of buckets?

- For a family service center, the buckets could be supporting individuals, strengthening families, and building community, or empowering youth, families, and the elderly.
- For a faith-based school: nurture the spirit, educate the mind, transform the community.
- For an environmental organization: protect, restore, preserve.
- For a cancer support organization: providing a community of support, empowerment, and hope.
- For a refugee resettlement organization: rescuing, nurturing, empowering.
- For an arts group: supporting artists, celebrating expression, engaging communities.

However you slice and dice your mission, the three buckets need to be large enough to contain all of your programs—you can't have any programs left out nor can you have more than three buckets.

As you look to assign each of your programs to a bucket, don't worry if some of your programs span all three buckets. For example at the faith-based school whose buckets are nurture the spirit, educate the mind, and transform the community, one of their programs is community service learning, where the students volunteer in local nursing homes. That community service program could conceivably fall under any of their three buckets.

While the buckets you choose may feel a bit awkward and confining to you at first, remember that they are meant to provide a framework for a newcomer to your organization to grasp conceptually all that you do. They are meant to make your work engaging and understandable to new people. We want people to be able to go home that night and tell some-

...if you are committed to getting it right, you must have only three buckets and every program you offer must fit into one of these three buckets.

one about your Point of Entry Event and succinctly state the three areas of impact and share a story or two.

During the initial Point of Entry Event, people will get an overview of these areas, including specific myth-buster facts, stories, and needs. From this introductory event, they will be able to decide if they want to learn more. In your subsequent contacts you will be able to go deeper into their particular areas of interest, which often follow their passion for one particular bucket area.

You will see many uses for the buckets as we go through each step of the Benevon Model. Remember: if you are committed to getting it right, you must have only three buckets and every program you offer must fit into one of these three buckets.

Customizing Your Mission Message

Once you've chosen your buckets, you can go back and write your Mission Message.

Answer these questions:

1. *What do you do?*
   For example, we educate children, we shelter families, we clean up rivers, we provide international relief.
2. *Who, where, and how many do you serve?*
   For example, 250 children in Smith County; 40 women and children in Missoula, Montana; over 1,000 families in sub-Saharan Africa each year; three rivers in northern Michigan.
3. *How do you accomplish this?* This is where you insert your three buckets.

Now put this all together into your Mission Message:

(Organization name) (what do we do) ____________ to/for (number of) ______________(people/animals/ rivers) __________________ in the (geographic area) ______________________ through/by (three buckets) ____________, ___________, and ____________.

For example, at Abilities in Action, we proudly serve 220 individuals who have physical challenges here in West Central Texas by promoting self-sufficiency, securing shelter, and ensuring mobility.

For a mentoring program: We create friendships for 200 people ages 3 to 93 in the greater Kansas City area every year by building caring relationships, celebrating dignity, and transforming lives.

For a behavioral health organization: We provide comprehensive mental health services to nearly 6,000 people in Jackson County by responding to needs, restoring lives, and building a healthy community.

Here is a worksheet to help you as you develop your buckets and your Mission Message.

MISSION MESSAGE TEMPLATE

What do you do? ____________________

Who and how many do you serve/ population/ geographic area? ____________________

____

What are the three ways you accomplish your larger mission? ____________________

Bucket 1	Bucket 2	Bucket 3
Programs/Services	Programs/Services	Programs/Services
______	______	______
______	______	______
______	______	______
______	______	______

Mission Message Template

(Organization name) ____________ (what do we do) ____________

to/for (number of) ____________ (people/animals/rivers) ____________

in the (geographic area) ____________

through/by (three buckets) ____________, ____________, and ____________.

Uses for Buckets

1. Overall Marketing: Buckets provide succinct "elevator speech"
2. Point of Entry: Making your work understandable to Point of Entry guests
3. Ask Event: Names of giving levels or examples of the impact
4. Free Feel-Good Cultivation Events: Can be themed to match buckets
5. Capital Campaign: Can name bucket area/program/building after the donor
6. Endowment Campaign: Donor can endow favorite bucket

Customizing Your Point of Entry Agenda

Now you are ready to integrate the buckets or areas of impact into the design of your Point of Entry.

POINT OF ENTRY AGENDA

1. To start
   a. Greeting
   b. Sign in
   c. Mix and mingle
2. Program
   a. While seated
      - Welcome (board member)
      - Visionary Leader Talk
      - Personal connection, results, vision for the future
   b. Tour: three stops
      - Each stop: Myth-Buster Fact, story, need
   c. Live testimonial
3. Thank you/wrap up

To Start

The first few minutes after your guests arrive and before your official Point of Entry Event program begins are critical to setting the tone.

Greeting

Each guest's experience begins with a greeting from a volunteer or one of your students right at the front door. The greeter welcomes the guests, takes their coats, and walks with them to the sign-in table.

The majority of your Point of Entry guests will have been invited to attend personally by a friend.

Sign-In: Capturing Names with Permission

The majority of your Point of Entry guests will have been invited to attend personally by a friend. They have been told that your organization is trying to spread the word in the community about its good work and that you are looking for feedback about how you are telling your story. They are told in advance that they will not be asked to give money at the event.

Therefore, when they arrive that first day, they know that they are coming to a one-hour introductory event. They are coming to check out your work at the recommendation of a trusted friend. They are predisposed to like you. They are willing to give you their basic contact information because the person who invited them also told them they would receive one follow-up phone call.

The Sign-In Table

The sign-in table is the essential checkpoint through which all visitors must pass. A friendly, detail-oriented staff person or volunteer gives your visitors a sign-in card and waits while they fill it out. The only information you have enough permission to gather at this early stage is their name, address, phone number (whichever one they want to give you), e-mail address, and the name of the person who invited them to the Point of Entry Event. If guests ask what this card is for, simply tell them that you would like to call them once to follow up and get their feedback about the event.

Here is a template to use for your sign-in card.

POINT OF ENTRY SIGN-IN CARD

To be filled out at check-in table upon arrival at Point of Entry.

Welcome!

Organization Logo

Point of Entry Name

Today's Date: ______________________________

Name: ______________________________

Address: ______________________________

City: ______________ State: __________ Zip: __________

Day Phone: ______________ Evening Phone: ______________

Email: ______________________________

Invited by: ______________________________

Brief Mix-and-Mingle Time

As the rest of the guests are gathering before your official start time, offer them a cup of coffee or tea (no food is necessary) and introduce them to other visitors. This is a good time for the executive director, board members, and the person who will be making the Follow-Up Calls to be available for informal conversations. Point out pictures on the walls, displays, scrapbooks, or any special features of the room they are in.

Program (while seated)

It is critical that everyone is seated during this first portion of the Point of Entry so they can focus on the program. People should sit around a common table, not in theater-style rows. For a classic Point of Entry Event, which is done in your office, you will have 10 to 15 guests. The speakers most likely

As with every speaker who follows, the guests need to know that this person genuinely cares.

will be seated right around the table with the guests to keep it feeling informal. There is no podium or stage, none of the speakers should be holding scripts or note cards. There is no video or PowerPoint. It should all feel very casual yet tightly crafted.

Placed on the conference table in front of each guest is a packet of handouts, including a Fact Sheet, your Wish List, and an optional simple brochure.

Welcome (3 minutes)

The program begins with a welcome greeting from a board member or volunteer, following this sample script:

"Thank you all for coming and thanks to the person who invited you here today (or to our Ambassador host, Sam).

"Our goal today is to give you a firsthand experience of the work of Abilities in Action. We hope today's session will educate and inspire you. As we go through the next hour together, please be thinking of anyone in your life who might want to learn more about our organization. Sue, who will be your tour guide today, will call you in the next week to get your feedback."

Then the welcome person tells their own personal story about why they work or volunteer with your organization. They might talk about a family member who benefited from a similar program or a childhood memory or incident. As with every speaker who follows, the guests need to know that this person genuinely cares. For example, one board member for a large organization serving people with intellectual and developmental disabilities shared that, growing up, his best friend Tom had a sister, Rita, with intellectual challenges and told how Tom struggled when friends would tease Rita or him. He shared in his welcome remarks that he felt he had learned so much from Tom and Tom's family that he wanted to help others dispel the myths as well. He said it was his greatest privilege to serve on this board.

What is it about the mission of this organization that so inspires them? Was there something in their own life that drew them to this?

Guest Introductions (5 minutes)

Next, if there are 10 guests or fewer, the welcome person asks each guest to introduce themselves and say what connection they have to your organization or your work. This should take no longer than five minutes. Sue (the person who will be making the Follow-Up Calls in our example above) and others on the team pay close attention for cues that will help to warm up the first Follow-Up Call.

For example, at a hospital Point of Entry Event, one guest said that he was new to town and had no formal connection to the hospital but wanted to come inside to visit in case he or his family needed services in the future. Another woman said that her mother and granddaughter had both been born at this hospital. A third gentleman said his wife had received cancer care there. Again, these simple statements can be wonderful ice-breakers for that first Follow-Up Call.

Visionary Leader Talk (5 minutes)

The Visionary Leader is the executive director or top-ranking paid staff member. If there are no paid staff members, the Visionary Leader is the person in the top volunteer role, usually the board chair.

The Visionary Leader speaks for five minutes. In the first two minutes, they tell why they chose this particular organization to work for. What is it about the mission of this organization that so inspires them? Was there something in their own life that drew them to this? Do they feel called to this organization's purpose? I recall a story from a CEO of a Red Cross chapter, whose family had immigrated to the U.S. when she was a child. When she was five, there was a fire in their apartment building in the middle of the night. Her memory of her parents' terror and helplessness, and the Red Cross volunteer who hugged her through it all and gave her a warm blanket, stuck with her all those years. Her goal as she entered the nonprofit field was always to give back to

What would it look like if the problem or issue your organization addresses were fully managed or eliminated altogether? Paint the grand picture for them.

the Red Cross. When she heard about the job opening, she knew it had her name on it!

Then for one minute, the Visionary Leader recounts some of the key accomplishments of the organization, focusing on real results in each of the three bucket areas. For example, "In the past five years, over 90% of the teenage offenders who have left our residential program have not reoffended. That compares with the national average of only 55%."

In the final two minutes, the Visionary Leader shares their vision for the future of the organization. Where do you want to be three years from now or five years from now? How many more people or communities will be served, how many more families housed, children educated? How will your advocacy efforts to streamline the foster care placement process be realized? How many children will have permanent homes as a result of your efforts?

Most Visionary Leaders have huge dreams for their organizations. Often their dreams are modulated by reality and by the time they talk about them out loud, they have watered them down to their more modest hopes and safe, attainable goals. That is not what we want in the Visionary Leader Talk. The guests at your Point of Entry Event will be hearing this for the first (and perhaps only) time. Tell them your bigger dreams! What would it look like if the problem or issue your organization addresses were fully managed or eliminated altogether? Paint the grand picture for them.

We spend a great deal of time coaching Visionary Leaders to speak succinctly and passionately, getting to the heart of their love of the work, not droning on about facts, statistics, and programs with acronyms that will numb the guests. The talk must make it clear to the guests that the Visionary Leader sees clearly where the organization is going and that the organization needs support from the community in order to get there. In other words, the Visionary Leader must convey a clear sense of "the gap," as well as their plan, even if only loosely defined, for filling that gap. And they must do this with genuine emotion.

Here is an outline of the Visionary Leader Talk.

VISIONARY LEADER TALK WORKSHEET FOR POINT OF ENTRY EVENTS

5 Minutes; 1,000 Words

Name of organization: ______________________________

I. Your personal story (2 min)

A. What specific personal incident or experience in your life brought you to this organization or this type of work? ______________________________

____

II. Today (Use your Fact Sheet to illustrate any key points) (1 min)

A. State your Mission Message:

____

B. Today you'll hear about three areas of our work, which are ______________, ______________ and ______________ .

C. Highlight one result/outcome from each bucket: (e.g., success rate; lives changed)

i. Bucket #1 ______________________________

ii. Bucket #2 ______________________________

iii. Bucket #3 ______________________________

III. Vision for the future (2 min)

A. Where do you want to be five to ten years from now? ______________________________

____

B. What is the gap to be filled to reach the vision? ______________________________

____

C. What three needs must be met to fill the gap? ______________________________

____

D. What will be the impact on the community when we fulfill on our vision? ______________

____

This tour—whether real or virtual—must include three stops, one for each bucket. A fourth stop is optional but must reference one of the three buckets.

Tour: Three Stops (30 to 40 minutes)

During the next 30 to 40 minutes of the program, guests take a tour of your mission.

Because it is essential that the person who will be making the official Follow-Up Calls is introduced at the Point of Entry and has a speaking role during this event, this follow-up person often serves as the tour guide and may also be the storyteller at one of the tour stops.

The first time this person speaks, often at the start of the tour, they tell briefly how and why they became involved with the organization. This brief talk must be memorable enough to inspire the guests to look forward to their follow-up phone call!

This tour—whether real or virtual—must include three stops, one for each bucket. A fourth stop is optional but must reference one of the three buckets.

Each Stop: Myth-Buster Fact, Story, Need

At each stop along the tour, you must dispel a myth with a myth-buster fact, share a story about a life that was changed, and tell an unmet need—something that money could buy—without asking for money. All of this must clearly connect to the bucket area.

For example, for their "self-sufficiency" tour stop, Abilities in Action might take people to the job training department where they see college students with severe physical disabilities taking a computer class. The instructor might come out to tell them that, although most people believe that even with an education, individuals with disabilities cannot join the workforce, the fact is that 95% of their students are placed in jobs where they stay five years or longer.

The tour guide ends by describing an unmet need.

Then she might tell the story of Louise, a former student who arrived at the center two years ago, with no job skills, despondent after her mother had died. Louise's trained, professional rehabilitation counselor, Eddie, arranged for job training for Louise, as well as an aide to help her get ready to go to work each morning, and the necessary ramps and transportation to accommodate her wheelchair. Best of all, Eddie arranged a great job for Louise at a company near her house. She has been there for over a year. In fact, she comes back to the center one night a week to help out in the computer training classroom and to inspire other students to keep going.

The tour guide ends by describing an unmet need. "As proud as we are of Louise, we have over 100 students on our waiting list right now, sitting at home, hoping we will call to give them an opportunity to get to work. We need one rehab counselor like Eddie for every 20 people on that waiting list."

Then the tour moves on to the "shelter" tour stop, about the housing program, where we again hear a myth-buster fact, a story, and a need. Sometimes the stories are told by staff, sometimes by reading a letter from a former client or a family member. The stories need to be short and powerful and each one told from a different perspective.

Crafting Your Essential Stories

We teach groups how to craft each story following what we call an Essential Story Template.

STAGES OF AN ESSENTIAL STORY

Stage	Elements	Suggested Phrasing
Stage 1: "Before"	Choose one person's story. Briefly describe their situation before working with your organization. What was their life like then? How difficult was it?	I'll never forget the story about Tom. Just a few years ago, Tom had a family and a job. Through a set of hard circumstances, he found himself hopeless and living under a bridge. He had fallen about as low as you can in our society. When I tell this story, it always reminds me of how much I take for granted in my own life, like a roof over my head, a hot shower every day, or even a hot meal. It is hard to imagine how he survived day-to-day.
Stage 2: "Intervention"	What brought this person into contact with your organization? What services and support did they receive from you? What was your personal observation of them at that time?	Someone mentioned to Tom that he could get a decent meal at our shelter. I will never forget the look in his eyes the first time he visited us. He was so embarrassed to have to take what he called a "handout." Every day Tom came to the shelter, he gained strength. He started to talk to others at the dinner table. We helped him learn computer skills so he was able to get a job in a new field. We provided hope for him. We helped him regain a sense of pride and self esteem. He was so proud of what he was accomplishing. I saw him in class one day tutoring one of the other new students who was struggling to learn to use the computer keyboard.
Stage 3: "After"	What are the results of the intervention? How has life changed for this person? What is now possible for them? What does this person now say about his/her life? How are they "giving back" to others?	Getting involved with our organization gave Tom a new future for his life. Tom is thriving now. He has an apartment, a job, and seems to be on top of the world. He volunteers with us when he has the time. He walked up to me a month or so ago, gave me a big hug and told me that our organization had literally saved his life. He drives by that bridge every now and then and it reminds him how lucky he is. He says he won't quit until everyone under that bridge gets the same chance he did. This is what people tell us all the time: "You people know no limits to caring."

You are telling guests precisely what your organization did to change a life. Include at least three specific services you provided.

The Stages of an Essential Story diagram above divides each story into three parts:

1. *Before:* Make sure you paint a strong visual picture of the person's life before they came to your organization. Often someone on your staff will recall that first day Mary walked in, what she looked like, how she carried herself, how old or how tall she was. Those are precisely the details that a Point of Entry guest needs to hear, yet they are often omitted from the story.

2. *Intervention:* Likewise, the Intervention is easy to skim over. This is the most important part! You are telling guests precisely what your organization did to change a life. Include at least three specific services you provided. Make sure the story is not told strictly in third person, as if being narrated by a storyteller. Rather, be sure to include the "voice" of the client or volunteer or theater patron, with a quote directly from them.

3. *After:* Tell the guests what are the results of your intervention. How has life changed for this person? What is now possible for them? What does this person now say about his/her life? How are they "giving back" to others?

This fill-in-the-blanks Essential Story Template is nearly foolproof for getting started with your first stories.

ESSENTIAL STORY TEMPLATE

1. Before ________ (name) found (came to, got involved with) ________ (our organization), her life was ________. So many of the things that you and I take for granted, such as ________, just weren't possible for ________ (name). It seemed to _______ that this would never change.

2. ________ found (came to, was referred to) ________ (our organization) by ________. Within ________ months (years), ________'s life turned around. Rather than ________, she was ________. Our ________ (specific, jargon-free) programs taught ________ to ________ and helped her get back on her feet again. People who saw ________ back then said she was ________ (a changed person, full of life again, able to look you in the eye). Really, what we provided her was ________ (a sense of pride, dignity, confidence, strength, courage) to get back out there and be a good ________ (parent, student).

3. Now, ________ is thriving. She has (is, does) ________. She says life will never be the same. Every time she thinks about (goes back to) ________, she says she thanks ________ for (giving her back her pride, her children, saving her life, her education, her dignity). The last time I saw her she was ________ (or: she came back to see us recently and said ________).

__________ is just one example of the lives that are being changed every day here at ________.

Have your board member or volunteer who opened the program be the person to wrap it up, following this sample script.

Live Testimonial (3 to 5 minutes)

End your tour with a live testimonial from someone whose life has been changed by your work. This can take place back in the conference room or at the door as people are ready to walk out. Make sure it follows the Essential Story format and is delivered powerfully. Your guests will never forget this.

Thank You and Wrap Up

Have your board member or volunteer who opened the program be the person to wrap it up, following this sample script.

"Thank you again for joining us today. We truly appreciate you taking the time to come and learn about Abilities in Action.

"Sue will be calling each of you in the next few days to get your feedback. If you were inspired by what you've seen today, the best way you can help us is by telling others, and inviting them to a similar Action Today Tour (Point of Entry).

"If you would like to invite others or host a session like this for a group of your own friends or colleagues, please let Sue know that when she calls you. Thank you all and have a great day!"

Resist the temptation to have a question and answer session with the whole group at the end. It is far better to debrief with your guests one-on-one by phone in the next few days after they have digested what they saw. Of course, if people want to linger individually at the door with a few more questions or comments, that is fine.

This Point of Entry Worksheet should help you to outline all that we have covered so far.

POINT OF ENTRY WORKSHEET

1. Greeter (title): ____________________
2. Sign-in/handout person (title): ____________________
3. Mix & mingle activities: ____________________
4. Agenda: ____________________
   a. Welcome (board member/volunteer): (3 min) ____________________
   b. Visionary Leader (executive director/CEO): (5 min) ____________________
   c. Tour (walk around): Real _____ Virtual _____ (30-40 min) Tour guide: ____________________

      Bucket 1: ____________________ Tour stop 1: ____________________
      Myth/Stereotype: ____________________
      Fact: ____________________
      Story: ____________________ Perspective: ____________________
      Need: ____________________
      Bucket 2: ____________________ Tour stop 2: ____________________
      Myth/Stereotype: ____________________
      Fact: ____________________
      Story: ____________________ Perspective: ____________________
      Need: ____________________
      Bucket 3: ____________________ Tour stop 3: ____________________
      Myth/Stereotype: ____________________
      Fact: ____________________
      Story: ____________________ Perspective: ____________________
      Need: ____________________
      Optional tour stop 4: ____________________ Bucket: ____________________
      Myth/Stereotype: ____________________
      Fact: ____________________
      Story: ____________________ Perspective: ____________________
      Need: ____________________

   d. Final testimonial person/story: (3-5 min) ____________________
   e. Closing remarks (title): (2 min) ____________________
5. Follow-up and tracking: ____________________
   a. Title of person who will ensure that all Benevon Follow-Up Calls are made within one week and that notes are entered into data tracking system (this person must attend Point of Entry):
      ____
   b. Name of data tracking system you will use: ____________________
6. Dates and times of next 12 Point of Entry Events : ____________________

You will notice there is no video or PowerPoint used at a Point of Entry Event.

Final Considerations

We still have a few more questions to answer before you will be able to complete your Point of Entry Worksheet.

Selecting Your Speakers

Initially, the speakers for your Point of Entry Event will include the:

- Welcome person—a board member or the Ambassador hosting this event
- Visionary Leader—CEO or executive director
- Development director or person who will be making the Follow-Up Calls after each Point of Entry—this person often serves as the tour guide
- Testimonial speaker

Over time, you may find ways to streamline the number of people needed to produce your Point of Entry Events. For example, the board member might also be the testimonial speaker at the end of the program, if they have a personal story to share.

High Touch/Low Tech

You will notice there is no video or PowerPoint used at a Point of Entry Event. It is intentionally designed to be more informal, high-touch, and person-to-person, as if a group of close friends are sitting around a table talking about something they all care about. Do not be tempted to deviate from this format if you want your Point of Entry to sizzle.

The Venue

The preferred Point of Entry venue is your organization's main office or site. This gives people the visual experience of your work and has them feel more connected. We find that people will remember you best if they have physically been to your site.

If you are concerned about the confidential nature of what people might see on a tour, there are ways to highlight only the programs or clients you want them to see.

Even if you think there would not be much for people to see at your office, there is a lot you can do to spruce it up and turn it into the perfect venue for a Point of Entry. You can add photos to the walls and tell a story about what goes on in each room as you walk people through. Stopping by the desk of a hard-working staff person to have them share an anecdote about someone who has benefited from their program will make a big impact, as will having someone read a testimonial letter from a grateful former client in your conference room.

If you are concerned about the confidential nature of what people might see on a tour, there are ways to highlight only the programs or clients you want them to see. Stories can be told by staff or by reading letters from clients and family members. It is even possible to put on your Point of Entry in one room, without ever walking people through the facility. By using photos and live testimonials, you can paint a powerful picture that people will never forget.

Ideal Size

The ideal size for a regularly scheduled, on-site Point of Entry is somewhere between 10 and 15 people. This allows for personal interaction and a manageable follow-up schedule.

Handouts at Your Point of Entry Event

Guests will receive two handouts plus, optionally, your organization's basic brochure.

1. Fact Sheet

   Front side:

   - Mission Message
   - Three Buckets: each with example of myth, fact, client quote, need
   - Pie chart of people served and/or revenue

Your first consideration should be the time of day that is most convenient for your guests.

Back side:

- Wish List
  a. Small to large
  b. 10 items maximum
  c. Things you really want
  d. Volunteer positions
  e. No prices or monetary amounts

2. Card with dates of future Point of Entry Events

3. Brochure—basic version *(optional)*

Timing

Your full Point of Entry Event should last one hour—no longer.

Deciding when to have your Point of Entry Events takes experimentation and depends on where they will be held. Your first consideration should be the time of day that is most convenient for your guests. If you are asking them to come to an out-of-the-way location, what time of day is easiest for them to get there? Working people might prefer early morning, late in the day, or lunchtime. Stay-at-home parents and retired people may prefer midday.

Next, consider the best time to show them your programs or take them on your tour. If you are planning to include live testimonials from staff or program participants, what times of day are those programs in session? Even within the work day, there may be certain times when there is more to see than others, for example, times when the kids are the freshest or the volunteers are the busiest. Many arts organizations will hold their Point of Entry Events in conjunction with a rehearsal or preview showing, which dictates the best dates and times. Weeknights in people's living rooms often work well for grassroots and women's organizations.

One organization that serves abused children calls their Point of Entry "If These Walls Could Talk."

Finally, after testing various times, many groups decide to offer their regularly scheduled Point of Entry Events at two alternating times each month—for example, one in the morning and one in the early afternoon—to make them convenient and accessible for everyone.

Naming Your Point of Entry Event

Take the time to choose a clever, inviting name for your Point of Entry. *The term "Point of Entry" is for your internal use only*. It is much too clinical to use with the general public.

One Benevon workshop participant team from an organ-donor program named their Point of Entry Events "Lifesaver Events." One Red Cross chapter named theirs "The Red Cross Experience." One organization that serves abused children calls their Point of Entry "If These Walls Could Talk." A Girl Scout council calls theirs "Beyond the Cookie Box." Other groups call their Points of Entry names such as "Meet Family Services," "Getting to Know Your Humane Society," "Village Theater 101," or "Touching Lives Tour." Find something unique and clever that reflects your mission and relates to your three buckets.

Frequency

You should be putting on Point of Entry Events two times per month with 10 to 15 people in attendance. Therefore, choose a venue and time of day that can work on a repetitive basis, such as the first Wednesday morning and the third Thursday afternoon of each month.

Having to muster up new tour guides, speakers, and stops on the tour each month is a recipe for failure.

Making Your Point of Entry Events Sustainable

We tell the groups in our Sustainable Funding Program that once they adopt the Benevon Model, they should assume they will be putting on Point of Entry Events for the rest of their organization's life! That becomes a powerful wake-up call to everyone to be sure that each element is sustainable. Having to muster up new tour guides, speakers, and stops on the tour each month is a recipe for failure. It may take you up to 12 Point of Entry Events to experiment with the best format, time of day, venue, etc. But once you get it right, don't change a thing.

CHAPTER 11

STEP EIGHT: KEYS TO SUCCESSFUL FOLLOW-UP

In the Benevon Model, follow-up is the glue that holds the whole model together. When your goal is to build lifelong relationships with individual donors, the follow-up process never ends. Whether after the initial Point of Entry Event or after each subsequent donor contact, you will be asking your donors for their personal feedback and listening closely for clues as to how they might like to become more involved.

The first Benevon Follow-Up Call, which happens after the initial Point of Entry Event, is not just a polite thank-you call, in which case it could be made by the Ambassador or the person who invited each guest to attend. It is fine for the Ambassador to call their guest to thank them for coming. However, the official Follow-Up Call must be made by someone representing the organization, someone to whom the guest can give candid feedback, without any sense of obligation to the friend who invited them.

The purpose of the Follow-Up Call is to discover whether or not this person is interested in becoming more involved with your organization. If the guest does want to become more involved, the Follow-Up Call is the opportunity to determine the particular aspects of your work that most inspire them and who else they may want to invite to attend a Point of Entry Event.

This person needs to enjoy building relationships—and talking on the telephone!

If you discover during the Follow-Up Call that the guest does not want to get involved, the guest is "blessed-and-released," but not until you have asked if there is anyone else they might want to invite to a future Point of Entry Event.

Selecting the Ideal Person to Make the Follow-Up Calls

As you begin implementing the Benevon Model, it is worth thinking through who will be responsible for making these critical Follow-Up Calls.

The official Follow-Up Call should be made by the one staff member who is the Team Leader accountable for the successful implementation of the Benevon Model within the organization. This person needs to enjoy building relationships—and talking on the telephone! This person will be each guest's ongoing primary contact at the organization and will guide the cultivation process leading up to the Ask Event and beyond.

The ideal Follow-Up Call person must:

- Attend every Point of Entry Event and have a speaking role, either as the tour guide, storyteller, or testimonial speaker
- Enjoy talking to people on the phone
- Be accountable for Ambassador recruitment and oversee the Ambassador Manager
- Have access to the executive director or CEO to get responses to donors' questions or ideas in a timely manner
- Possess the maturity and ability to interact with all types of people
- Enjoy developing relationships with people over time
- Be detail-oriented and committed to tracking every donor conversation in your database

She chats informally with as many guests as possible before the event begins, asking questions like, "How did you hear about us?"

Setting Up the Follow-Up Calls for Success

As your guests are leaving the Point of Entry Event—inspired, informed, and rushing off to their next appointment—the person who will be making the Follow-Up Call says to each of them, "Thank you for coming. I'll give you a call later this week to get your feedback."

Now let's look at what must happen before, during, and after the Point of Entry to set up each Follow-Up Call very naturally for success.

Before the Point of Entry Program Begins

Review the guest list. Make sure the primary person who will be making the Follow-Up Calls (Sue, in our prior example) knows each guest by name or, at a minimum, knows the name of the person who invited each guest.

Sue stands in the reception area near the sign-in table and greets each guest warmly as they arrive: "Welcome to Hope House. I'm Sue, the one you talked to on the phone!" Note that Sue is not the official greeter stationed at the front door of the building, nor is she the official sign-in person who is stationed at the table to be sure each guest fills out a guest card. She has the flexibility to move around. She chats informally with as many guests as possible before the event begins, asking questions like, "How did you hear about us?"

Five minutes before the program is scheduled to begin, Sue ushers the guests into the meeting room and asks them to take a seat at the table.

Set aside time, immediately following each Point of Entry Event, to meet with your team to go through the guest cards and decide who will make each Follow-Up Call.

During the Point of Entry Event

A board member or volunteer opens the program following the script on page 122, welcoming the guests, introducing Sue, sharing their own story, and (if there are 10 guests or fewer) asking guests to introduce themselves including what connection, if any, they have to the organization.

During the tour portion of the Point of Entry, Sue serves as the tour guide or story teller at one of the tour stops, first introducing herself by sharing her personal connection to the organization.

At the end of the Point of Entry Event, the same board member or volunteer who made the opening remarks thanks people for coming and reminds them that Sue will be calling each of them in the next few days to get their feedback, including their ideas for who else they might know who would want to attend a future Point of Entry Event.

Immediately Following the Point of Entry Event

Set aside time, immediately following each Point of Entry Event, to meet with your team to go through the guest cards and decide who will make each Follow-Up Call. For the most part, these calls will all be made by your designated staff Follow-Up Call person. If you have a prominent person or elected official, a board member or major donor, whom you feel would respond better to receiving a Follow-Up Call from the CEO directly, this is the time to make these important call assignments. Remember, whoever makes the first Follow-Up Call will be responsible for the ongoing relationship with this guest.

Consider yourself a detective on a mission to determine how each person might like to become involved, even if only a little bit, with your organization.

When to Make the Official Post-Point of Entry Follow-Up Call

The ideal time to make your Follow-Up Calls is on the second or third day following the Point of Entry Event. Technically, we say you can make these calls within one week of the event, but sooner is better. Give the guests a day or two to digest what they experienced and yet not so long that they will have forgotten the impact of the event.

What to Have on Hand when Making the Follow-Up Call

Be sure that the Follow-Up Call person has on hand a copy of the Wish List (see page 135) each guest will have received at the Point of Entry. This list should include several volunteer opportunities, starting with Ambassadors, as well as 8 to 10 tangible items you really need.

Also, you will need a copy of the Ambassador Invitation Script nearby (see page 84).

The Detailed Follow-Up Call Script

Think of this as a research call with a specific list of points to be covered. Consider yourself a detective on a mission to determine how each person might like to become involved, even if only a little bit, with your organization. It has to be a custom-fitted type of involvement, tailored to their needs and interests. You must have your radar detector turned up to high intensity for this call. You are listening for clues. You may need to practice asking people questions and then not talking so you can listen closely to the essence of what they are saying as well as what they are not saying.

Here is a more detailed outline of the Five-Step Follow-Up Call that will be helpful to have nearby when you make these calls.

BENEVON DETAILED FIVE-STEP FOLLOW-UP CALL

1. Thank you for coming.

2. What did you think?
   - Of the stories you heard?
   - What area of our work most interested you? Was it (bucket #1, #2, or #3)?
   - What new thoughts or ideas did you come away with?
   - Do you have a personal connection to our work? Tell me about it.
   - Did you leave with any questions I can answer for you?
   - What advice do you have for us?

3. Be quiet and listen.
   - Take notes on what they say.
   - Enter notes into database.

4. Is there any way you can see yourself becoming involved with us?
   - Invite others to Point of Entry Events.
   - Have a list of things people could do, such as volunteer opportunities; making reminder calls for Points of Entry; or volunteering (e.g., tutoring or mentoring a child).
   - Reference the Wish List items.
   - Host a Point of Entry or a Point of Entry in a Box.
   - Become an Ambassador.
   - Activity related to their bucket area of interest (e.g., meet with the program director or tour the facility, invite to a small event).

5. Is there anyone else you can think of that we ought to invite to a Point of Entry?
   - Who else in your daily life? Other groups you participate in, etc.?
   - Maybe a family member, someone you work with or a friend?
   - Someone you know who has a personal connection or a real passion for our work.
   - Example: "You mentioned you work in the healthcare field. Is there anyone else from your work —or from your book club, for that matter—who you think should know about our work?"

Here is a suggested script for the Follow-Up Call, including the points to be covered:

Point 1: "Thank you for coming."
"Hello, Maria. It was great meeting you at the tour of the children's home earlier this week. I was calling to thank you for taking the time to come out and visit us. It means a great deal to us that you took your time to do that.

"As we said there, we are offering these tours as a way to tell our story to more people in the community, to expand the base of folks who know what we're doing. We'd really appreciate your feedback."

Point 2: "What did you think?"
"What did you think of what you learned, what you heard, what you saw?" Most people's first response will be to tell you something polite but nonspecific.

This is where the brief self-introductions you heard at the Point of Entry Event will come in handy, to break the ice.

"I recall you said your family was new to the area and that you had been very involved as a board member and former dancer with a similar dance group when you were living in Colorado. What kind of dance were you doing there?"

Ask more questions. Ask for advice. Get them talking.

"We have really struggled getting that new ethnic dance program off the ground. How did you get the word out to your desired audience in your former program?

"How do you think we did at telling the story of the young boy who was just introduced to dance or the grandmother who was so proud to be participating in the movement class?

"How could we be doing a better job of telling our story?"

But what if the guest is on the fence?

Point 3: Be quiet and listen.
Pause and let them talk as long as they like. As you are listening closely to their response, pick up on any cues or hot buttons that interest them. Add a bit more information about programs they like. If they don't offer anything more, and they have not told you that they absolutely are not interested, you can ask the next question.

Point 4: "Is there any way you could see yourself becoming involved with our organization?"
Notice in their response what kind of involvement they are looking for. Is it something very hands-on and tangible? A project, perhaps? An in-kind donation? Or do they prefer more of an arms-length advisory or referral role? All of these qualify as involvement.

If the guest is interested in becoming involved, listen closely for which aspect of your work they are most interested in, and suggest any relevant items on your Wish List. Often guests will bring up specific items, like, "I noticed you need some used computers. We are upgrading our office and have several we could donate." Or, "I belong to a group of real estate agents who are always looking to get involved in community projects. Maybe I could do what my friend Bob did and become one of your Ambassadors and bring our whole real estate group out for a tour. Would that work?"

If someone expresses an interest in becoming an Ambassador, follow the Ambassador Invitation Script on page 84.

But what if the guest is on the fence? Let's say they are hinting that they'd like to stay involved, perhaps they don't have much time, and they ask that you "keep me on your list."

No problem. Remind them that you have Point of Entry Events twice a month and encourage them to come back with a friend or send a friend. Perhaps they mentioned at the start of the event when they introduced themselves that they work in human resources at the local power company. You could

Many people will have a hard time telling you they are not interested in becoming involved, even though that is their preference.

refer back to that now. "I remember you mentioning your work at the power company. Do you ever have community groups come out to do presentations for your employees? We do a lot of that. We can take our _______ (Point of Entry) on the road."

That may lead to a referral to the person in charge of such presentations at their company or the ability to host a private Point of Entry Event in your offices for a group of their employees. In that very natural interaction, you have identified an informal Ambassador, someone who has a natural group of people they could invite to your Point of Entry Event.

When to Bless-and-Release

Many people will have a hard time telling you they are not interested in becoming involved, even though that is their preference. They do not want you to think they are mean and uncaring. Therefore, it is critical that the person making each Follow-Up Call listens carefully to read the signals from a guest who is trying to tell you "No." What might these signals look like? They include hesitating, being polite but not forthcoming with any suggestions or responses, being quiet or noncommittal. If you are listening closely during the Follow-Up Call, you will start to develop radar for those guests who are nicely asking you to "bless-and-release" them. Thank them for their time and ask them to keep your organization in mind, and then put a note in their file in your database saying you have blessed-and-released them. *Do not put them on your mailing lists or attempt to contact them further*. In the long run, they will respect you a lot more for valuing their time and involvement in other organizations.

However, even if the person does not want to become involved, before you bless-and-release them, don't forget to ask them the last question:

Do not put this guest on your mailing list or follow up with them in any way after this, unless they request it.

Point 5: "Is there anyone else you would suggest we invite to another______ (Point of Entry Event) like the one you attended?" If they give you a name, ask, "May I ask you to call the person first to let them know I will be calling?"

Any suggestions, names, or ideas they have given you need to be acted on immediately and, in turn, reported back to them quickly.

If you do not connect: leave two phone messages and send one e-mail message, then note in your database that you have blessed-and released this person. Do not put this guest on your mailing list or follow up with them in any way after this, unless they request it.

Track All Contacts in Database

Anyone making a Follow-Up Call, or having any donor contact, must enter all notes into the database faithfully. Be sure to set a reminder in your tracking system for the date of your next contact.

The Start of a Long-Term Relationship

As we conclude this chapter on follow-up, here are a few observations about today's donors:

- They want to get involved in meaningful ways.
- They want to call the shots.
- They want to control the pace of their relationship with you.
- They are prepared to be loyal.
- They appreciate a direct and honest answer more than a superficial, albeit polite, response.
- They are looking for the perfect blend of their talents and resources with your needs. And so are you!

The Follow-Up Call is your ticket to customizing the ideal type of involvement for each donor. It is the start of that long-term relationship.

CHAPTER 12

STEP NINE: NAVIGATING THE CULTIVATION SUPERHIGHWAY

In the Benevon Model, the part of the circle between Step Two: Follow Up and Involve, and Step Three: Asking for Money, is what we call the Cultivation Superhighway. Everything that happens between your organization and the donor or potential donor in this part of the circle is designed to hasten the ripening of the fruit that will be ready to be picked by Step Three.

Contacts on the Cultivation Superhighway

It is contacts that accelerate the pace on the Cultivation Superhighway. There is a direct correlation between the number of contacts you have with a potential donor along this Superhighway and the size of their gifts.

People often ask, "How many contacts should we have with a potential donor along the Superhighway before we can ask them for money?"

The answer is that there is no prescribed right number or type of contacts. The purpose of these contacts is to deepen the donor's involvement with your organization based on a natural give-and-take of information. The ideal number and sequence of contacts is so customized to the unique needs and interests of each donor that you may feel as though your donors are cultivating themselves through the process.

By personal, we mean that each contact must be one-on-one, speaking only to them, making each donor feel special. It can't feel generic.

The Definition of Personal Contact

The four key conditions to remember are that each contact must be:

1. *Personal*
2. *Structured as a dialog* and delivered through each donor's preferred medium
3. *Relevant* to the donor's unique interests and needs
4. *Timed* to the pace and style of the donor

It follows, then, that the better someone within your organization knows each donor, the more successful they will be at determining the most appropriate type and frequency of contact.

Let's examine each of these conditions further.

Personal

By personal, we mean that each contact must be one-on-one, speaking only to them, making each donor feel special. *It can't feel generic.* It can't feel so standard and impersonal that the donor knows that this identical contact is being made with every other donor, even though sometimes that may be the case. Each communication has to be customized enough that the donor knows you are speaking only to them, and you know what they need in order to feel special.

Think about what your organization is currently doing to stay in contact with your donors. Most groups tell us that the majority of their time is spent in the least personal types of contacts—sending out the newsletter via bulk mail, the expensive printed invitations to which only a fraction of people respond, the formal thank-you letter that engenders no next contact, or the direct-mail solicitation that keeps the relationship safely at arm's length.

It needs to be customized enough so that the donor knows you are speaking only to them. That is what will have each donor feel special.

Imagine if you were to take all the time and energy that your group puts into those impersonal contacts and instead refocused on getting to know one subset of your donors and supporters personally—for example, your direct mail donors who give more than $500 per year—by cultivating your relationship with them over time. Then it would feel very different to ask them for money, year after year. It would be far more satisfying to you and to the donors, and it would honor the mission of your organization, rather than entertaining, manipulating, and pressuring people to give.

Even if you didn't want to take the time to cultivate each of your donors one-by-one, face-to-face, you could at least begin with the people who have been dutifully giving—even small amounts—year after year, and begin to personalize those newsletters, invitations, and thank-you mailings to them, adding a handwritten note from someone who knows them and knows their particular interest in your organization.

Again, the first element in our definition of "personal" is that each contact must feel personal—it can't be generic. It needs to be customized enough so that the donor knows you are speaking only to them. That is what will have each donor feel special.

The classic example of this type of personal contact is the official Follow-Up Call we discussed in Chapter 11 that takes place three to five days after the potential donor's attendance at a first Point of Entry Event. Guests are told several times throughout the Point of Entry program that they would be receiving one Follow-Up Call. The Follow-Up Call follows a prescribed format of open-ended questions, beginning with thanking the potential donor for coming and then asking for their feedback. By asking for their input and truly listening to what they have to say, you have begun the dialog, the give and take.

There is no substitute for in-person, face-to-face communication.

Structured as a Dialog

To qualify as "personal" in the Benevon Model, each contact must allow for immediate dialog. This would include contacts that are made face-to-face, by phone, or online, so that the donor can respond right in the process of the contact.

There is no substitute for in-person, face-to-face communication. It allows for the immediate give-and-take we are looking for in a true dialog. It allows you to shake hands, make eye contact, read body language. It also lets you listen, clarify, refine, and respond to each question and concern the donor may have, right there in the moment.

However, the simplest and most efficient form of cultivation contact is still a telephone call. Whether the purpose of the call is to inform, invite, ask, thank, or just to say hello, the telephone is second only to face-to-face interaction in terms of allowing for a true dialog, letting you notice and use voice inflection, read pauses or sense hesitations, and pick up subtle expressions of interest.

Even if you don't reach the donor every time, once you get comfortable with leaving specific messages (the same way you do for friends and family members when you know they care enough to call you back), you will see the efficiency of these telephone contacts.

So, before you pick up the pen to write a letter, pick up the telephone. It is by far the most efficient form of personal contact for keeping this level of personal dialog going.

After face-to-face and telephone contact, online communication is a close third. Not the blanket spam type of e-mails we all rush to delete. Rather, the personal e-mail and Facebook messages we reply to first. E-mail allows for immediate dialog and can be extremely personal if customized.

Engage in dialog with your donors using their preferred method and don't hesitate to mix your media. Think of the many ways you communicate online.

Several of the smart CEOs we work with send out regular, highly customized e-mail to all their Multiple-Year Donors…

It's almost embarrassing for me to admit that my close relationship with my eighty-nine-year-old mother-in-law is based largely on back and forth e-mail, nearly daily. It is an ideal medium that allows for her hearing loss and my travel schedule. We really are able to connect personally this way. We also talk by phone once or twice a week and visit in person several times a year.

My twenty-something children communicate with me mostly via text message and phone, rarely e-mail. They both have active Twitter accounts that I follow and I often reply to their updates personally via direct message. I also subscribe to receive an automatic copy of their most recent blog posts, which I often use to trigger a conversation via direct e-mail or by posting a comment.

Turning back to how you communicate with your donors, here's another example.

Several of the smart CEOs we work with send out regular, highly customized e-mail to all their Multiple-Year Donors, either in an e-newsletter format or personal one-on-one e-mails. Of course, this is in addition to one-on-one donor meetings and personal phone calls.

Some CEOs will take that to another level in special circumstances, such as they did after Hurricane Katrina, reflecting the sheer desperation of the situation, sending daily, and then weekly, e-mail updates to all of their major donors. While these clearly were not customized to every individual in the group of donors, they were still very personal letters, often written late at night by an exhausted CEO, seeking moral support from his own constituents as much as anything. They were kind of an e-mail version of a narrative Wish List. While the senders never came out and asked for money outright, they clearly left the reader ready to write the check—and wanting to forward the e-mail on to others who could help fulfill some of the specific "Wish List" items needed.

As you get to know your donors well enough to anticipate their preferences and interests, you will know the natural next step they would like to take with you.

Relevant

By relevant, we mean relevant to the donor's self-interest. What is that donor's specific "hot button" about your organization? Once you know the answer to that question, rather than focusing on the most critical needs from your organization's point of view, each donor contact should focus on whatever "bucket" or area of impact interests your donor most.

As you get to know your donors well enough to anticipate their preferences and interests, you will know the natural next step they would like to take with you.

For example, a donor whose mother is living in your faith-based retirement community and is concerned with her safety might appreciate being invited to a planning meeting to talk about the new ramps and railings you are planning to install.

A health research organization could invite their donor to meet individually or in a group of donors with a research scientist who is working on the disease they have expressed a particular interest in.

This focus on relevance should also relieve you of the burden of sending out blanket invitations to events that are not of interest to all your donors and could, in fact, be off-putting to many of them.

Timed to the Pace and Style of the Donor

Each of us operates at our own pace, some faster, some slower. Thinking again of your friends and family; you know whose e-mails, text messages, or phone calls you must reply to right away versus those you can take a little longer to get back to. The same is true of your donors. Start by presuming that a two-day response time will be about right. As you learn each donor's unique pace, you can adjust this to be faster or slower.

You see that you could actually contribute some of the things on that list, but you are too busy to pick up the phone and call them or you might not want to appear that "forward."

From the Donor's Point of View

Let's stop for a minute and consider this picture from the donor's point of view.

Imagine yourself as one of the guests at your organization's Point of Entry Event. You've had just this one contact with the organization and you were impressed.

Now what?

They didn't ask you for money. They sent you home with some materials. You take a minute to read them. How interesting. There is an easy-to-read Wish List of all kinds of things they need. There are little items like toothbrushes, shampoo, pots and pans, help in the office once a week. And there are some medium-sized items like old computers, carpeting for the youth room, a van, math tutors. The list goes all the way up to the really big stuff: a new gymnasium, an underwriter for their international conference, a new office building, a properly staffed reading program.

You see that you could actually contribute some of the things on that list, but you are too busy to pick up the phone and call them or you might not want to appear that "forward." You put away the Wish List and go on to the next activity in your day.

Two days later, you get a phone call from Sue, that nice staff person you met at the tour or lunch meeting. She is thanking you for taking your time to come and asking for your input. "What did you think of our program?" You tell her in a reserved way how impressed you were. You mention that the intercultural studies program was especially appealing. At some point she asks, "Is there any way you could see yourself becoming involved?"

You may be thinking about underwriting that international conference. After all, it links to many other interests of yours, yet you don't want to lead off with something so big. "I notice you need some old computers," you respond. "I could help you with that."

Those old computers that had been cluttering the back room at the office are now front and center, with eager, curious children and their parents clicking away.

Sue is very appreciative and tells you immediately how much they are needed and for what program. The demand has increased so much that the computer lab is now open every evening and there are still people who can't get the computer time they need. My goodness, you are thinking, my old computers could really make a difference. We've upgraded our system at the office and those old ones are actually in the way. I'd be a real hero if I found a good cause to donate them to.

"Would it help if we came to pick them up?" she offers. "I know how happy it will make the people in the computer lab to have them before the next round of classes start." Before you know it, they have picked up the computers and you are getting a call inviting you to come back and see the expanded computer program in action one evening when it is in full swing. "Feel free to invite anyone else you'd like," offers that same warm, efficient staff person.

You arrive with your husband and two work colleagues just to check it out on your way to dinner. You are dazzled. Those old computers that had been cluttering the back room at the office are now front and center, with eager, curious children and their parents clicking away. The head of the computer program, a brainy looking fellow, happens to be there in the midst of all the action. He can't thank you enough.

Of course, as part of the evening's show-and-tell at the computer center, your low-key guide points out the students from the intercultural program, communicating with their international "e-pals." "It's just a start," she says. "They're always hungry for more real connections with other cultures." You go off to dinner with your friends. Everyone is feeling good, and you are looking like the person of the hour. For your friends, this was a pre-Point of Entry Event; for you it was a validation that you picked a winner.

You find yourself telling her that one of your friends is a teacher and asked if he could learn more.

The next week, the same nice staff person calls back to thank you for coming out again and for bringing those friends. "I hope they enjoyed seeing the program." she says enthusiastically. You find yourself telling her that one of your friends is a teacher and asked if he could learn more. And those work colleagues who came to the center and then to dinner have spread the word to a few others in the international department at the office. They're wondering if someone from the program could come out to talk with them about what they do. Before you know it, you find yourself checking calendars and arranging a date for a Point of Entry in a Box (Chapter 16) at your offices, and you're supplying the lunches!

And so it goes. A one-time visit to a Point of Entry Event and an effective Follow-Up Call lead to the birth of an in-kind gift, a volunteer, an Ambassador and—down the road—a new major donor. This is why we call it the Cultivation Superhighway.

CHAPTER 13

STEP TEN: THE ONE-ON-ONE ASK—SECURING YOUR FIRST LEADERSHIP, CHALLENGE, AND SPONSORSHIP GIFTS

Two key elements of a successful first-year implementation of the Benevon Model are having a Leadership or Challenge Gift secured before your Free One-Hour Ask Event as well as securing a sponsorship gift. These gifts will be good sources of both cash and confidence as you walk into your Ask Event.

However, the real reason we require the groups we work with to have these gifts to announce at their Ask Event is to train them in the process of cultivating and asking an individual donor for a gift.

Since the Benevon Model is, ultimately, a major gifts model, over time the majority of your financial results will come from one-on-one asking for increasingly larger gifts, rather that asking solely at the Ask Event.

Your upcoming first Ask Event will be a good impetus to motivate you to develop or refine these skills.

Leadership and Challenge Gifts Defined

Although we refer to these gifts as if they are the same kind, there are subtle differences. Both Leadership and Challenge Gifts are larger gifts, coming from one donor or a group of

Similar to a Leadership Gift, a Challenge Gift, which is sometimes referred to as a matching gift, is also a large sum of money announced right before the pitch.

donors. Although they may be grants from foundations, we prefer that these gifts come from individual donors, as a way to have our groups learn the process of cultivating and asking an individual donor for a major gift.

A Leadership Gift is a large sum of money that is announced right before the pitch at the Ask Event to inspire additional giving. It should send the message to the audience that your organization is worthy of major support and has already garnered that support from one or more generous donors.

Similar to a Leadership Gift, a Challenge Gift, which is sometimes referred to as a matching gift, is also a large sum of money announced right before the pitch. However, a Challenge Gift has some strings attached to it. Your donors decide what those stipulations are. Will their gift be used to match, dollar for dollar, every gift you receive on the day of the Ask Event? Will it be used to match every gift two-to-one? Perhaps they will want to match, specifically, gifts of those new donors who join your Multiple-Year Giving Society, pledging $1,000 or more for five years. Perhaps they will let you take all year to fulfill the full amount of the challenge. All of these stipulations need to be settled on in advance.

While they may seem a bit complicated up front, Leadership and Challenge Gifts can go a long way towards increasing your bottom line at your Ask Event and engaging major donors in your work.

LEADERSHIP AND CHALLENGE GIFTS

1. Sources
   a. One current donor
      - Individual
      - Family foundation
   b. Group of major donors
      - Board members
      - Current donors
      - Others
2. May be one-time gifts or pledges

For challenge gifts only:

3. Must decide what gets matched (e.g. Multiple-Year Giving Society gifts)
4. Has a deadline or time limit
5. Is announced and explained clearly at Ask Event

Deciding the Size of Your First Leadership or Challenge Gift

We require our groups to have, at a minimum, a Leadership or Challenge Gift the size of the five-year value of their middle giving level in their Multiple-Year Giving Society. Recall Chapter 8, where you chose either Option 1 or Option 2 for your three giving levels:

- Option 1: $1,000, $5,000, and $10,000 a year for the next five years
- Option 2: $1,000, $10,000, and $25,000 a year for the next five years

Therefore, your middle level would either be:

- In Option 1: $5,000 x 5 for a total Leadership or Challenge Gift of $25,000
- In Option 2: $10,000 x 5 for a total Leadership or Challenge Gift of $50,000

If you are using the lower giving levels in Option 1 above, your goal is to have a Leadership or Challenge Gift of $25,000 to announce at your Ask Event. We say you need to have at least four times your goal, or $100,000, in potential Asks, in order to reliably end up with $25,000 in gifts.

Use the form below to list out the possible sources of this gift, either by name (Mary Jones) or in broader categories (prior board members, prior major donors, or capital campaign donors). Look to all the categories of your Treasure Map.

LEADERSHIP / CHALLENGE GIFT PLAN

Total amount needed from Challenge Gift donors: $25,000

Potential donors to be cultivated and asked:

One current donor (individual or family foundation)	**Ask amount**
Mary Jones	5,000
Local retail store or vendor	5,000
Smith Family Foundation	20,000
Group of major donors	
Former board members	20,000
Prior one-year donors of $1,000+	25,000
Former capital campaign donors	25,000
Total $ (should equal four times the goal):	100,000

What are some of the signs people give to let you know they're getting ready to be asked?

Readiness Level

Looking over your list of potential donors for your Leadership or Challenge Gift, on a subjective readiness scale of 1 to 10, where 10 represents those most ready to be asked, how ready would you say each of these donors is to be asked for money right now?

You may be wondering how to determine the readiness level of a potential donor. If you think about it a bit, you'll realize you already have a well-developed radar for this. What are some of the signs people give to let you know they're getting ready to be asked?

1. They invite others to come to your events, such as Point of Entry Events.
2. They return your phone calls.
3. They answer your e-mails.
4. They ask for more information.
5. They ask questions.
6. They give you ideas and advice.
7. They volunteer, offer their time, show up, and help out.
8. They start talking about "we."
9. They tell others about you and refer others.
10. They make in-kind gifts of goods and services.

Rate each donor on your subjective readiness scale of 1 to 10.

Cultivation Plans

For each donor on your list, you will need to develop a Cultivation Plan.

Although you will not be able to predict exactly what each cultivation step will look like, you can certainly anticipate the next few steps in each donor's cultivation plan.

Next, choose one donor from this list who ranked at a readiness level of seven, eight, or nine. In other words, this donor is nearly ready to be asked, but might need a bit more cultivation to fully ripen the fruit.

Let's say the first donor from your list you've chosen to focus on is a woman named Rebecca. She is an executive at the local power company. She is single, no children, age 42. Your goal is to ask Rebecca for $10,000 towards your total Leadership/Challenge Gift of $25,000 for your after-school program, Great Kids. Using the plan format below, you would write in your goal of $10,000 in the goalpost near the top of the form.

Then starting at the bottom and working up the chart towards the Ask, list out the things that have already transpired with Rebecca. Her friend Irene, who is on your board and is an Ambassador, invited Rebecca to your stellar Point of Entry Event. When your development director, DeeDee, made the Follow-Up Call, Rebecca expressed real interest in the financial education program Great Kids offers. She is a big believer in young people learning about money and credit at an early age, having come from a very poor family herself. When DeeDee asks if there is any way that she could see herself becoming involved, Rebecca asks if Great Kids needs any volunteers to teach the financial education program.

CULTIVATION PLAN

Person to be asked: Rebecca
Asking for: $10,000
Cultivation Coordinator: DeeDee

$10,000

Action:	Date:	Outcome:
10.		
9.		
8.		
7. Meets with executive director, Ron, who thanks Rebecca, shares challenges & matching gift goal of $25,000	May 18	Makes $5,000 gift to be matched by her company; suggests other matching-gift donors
6. Meets DeeDee while volunteering	April 20	Asks about making a gift with corporate match
5. Receives Follow-Up Call	April 3	Shares feedback from employees
4. Hosts Point of Entry in a Box at her office	April 1	Power company's employees learn about Great Kids; Rebecca becomes more excited about the program.
3. Meets with program director, discusses learning aids	February 22	Signs on as volunteer & Ambassador
2. Receives Follow-Up Call	February 4	Expresses interest in financial education program
1. Attends Point of Entry Event as guest of friend Irene (Ambassador)	February 1	Learns about Great Kids; gets excited about at least one "bucket"

Notice that, although it sounds as if Rebecca is ready to be asked, DeeDee wisely waited...

DeeDee invites Rebecca back to meet with the person in charge of that program and they have a great connection, chatting away about the learning aids being used to teach the students. Rebecca signs on as a volunteer for one afternoon a week. As she becomes more involved, she talks with her friend, Irene, about what becoming an Ambassador entails. She then calls DeeDee back to offer to host a Point of Entry Event at her office as part of the brown-bag lunch series the power company offers once a month, where three local nonprofit organizations are invited in to offer simultaneous sessions about their work.

The last time Rebecca came in to volunteer, Rebecca asked DeeDee about making a gift to Great Kids. Her company will match her gift, which is very important to Rebecca, because it doubles the value to Great Kids. DeeDee thanked her for the generous offer and said she'd first like to have Rebecca meet her executive director, Ron, to learn more about what's going on at Great Kids. Rebecca agrees.

Notice that, although it sounds as if Rebecca is ready to be asked, DeeDee wisely waited, arranging one more cultivation contact, scheduled around an afternoon when Rebecca is at the center volunteering. During that meeting, the executive director, Ron, thanks Rebecca for all she has done, inquires about how her volunteer experience is going, acknowledges Irene for introducing Rebecca to Great Kids, and shares some of the successes and challenges facing the center. Being a savvy businesswoman, Rebecca has many questions. She is impressed with Ron's passion and his expertise.

By the end of the meeting, Rebecca is asking again how she can help financially. Knowing that Great Kids is looking for a $25,000 Challenge Gift to announce at the upcoming Ask Event, Ron starts talking with Rebecca about the

We like to say at Benevon that when the donor is ready, asking should be nothing more than nudging the inevitable.

upcoming event. He calls in DeeDee to help explain how the event will work and what Great Kids is hoping to raise at the event. Together, Ron and DeeDee share their goal of being able to announce the gift to be used as a match for the first $25,000 raised at the event. Rebecca jumps right in with questions and before Ron can ask her for a gift, she offers to give $5,000, which will be matched by her company. Furthermore, she names three other people from the power company that got very excited about Great Kids after the brown-bag lunch series. Rebecca offers to bring them out to see the center in person and work with Ron and DeeDee to secure the other $15,000 towards their $25,000 Challenge Gift. DeeDee and Ron are overjoyed as they say goodbye to Rebecca, thanking her sincerely for her support.

We like to say at Benevon that when the donor is ready, asking should be nothing more than nudging the inevitable.

As you design your Cultivation Plan for each donor, list out what has already transpired and then plan out the next possible step or two and watch the process unfold.

Let's back up and suppose that Rebecca hadn't been so forthcoming. She loved volunteering, hosted a Point of Entry Event at her office, but was too busy to do much more. How should Great Kids go about cultivating and asking her for that same $10,000?

DeeDee might call her up and invite her to meet with Ron, who has some new ideas about programming that he'd like her thoughts on.

In that same meeting, Ron could talk about challenges and plans, and spell out the needs for another staff member to supervise three volunteers who in turn could work with 10 students each. It may take two or three more visits or contacts back and forth before Rebecca is ready to be asked.

If you do not honestly know the answer, it is a good sign that you may need to have one or more cultivation contacts to find out the answers…

Pre-Ask Questions

The easiest way to determine donor readiness is to answer these Pre-Ask Questions for each donor.

As you go through this list, answer truthfully. Do not guess at your answers. If you do not honestly know the answer, it is a good sign that you may need to have one or more cultivation contacts to find out the answers to these questions before asking this donor for money. After all the good work you have been doing to gently get to know this donor and connect them to your organization's mission, it is far better to take the time to have these additional contacts, rather than rush into the Ask prematurely and risk alienating your donor.

Let's look at each question more closely.

1. *Exactly who will be asked?*
   Have you cultivated all of the key decision-makers? Should spouses, partners, children, parents, or business partners be included? Including them in the asking meeting or call tells them you respect their "vote" in the process. Down the road, one of these other people may become your main donor.

2. *Who will do the asking?*
   Will it be one person or more? Are these the most appropriate people to be asking this particular donor? Would another board member enhance the asking team? Is the asker too closely connected to the donor? Who is this donor's favorite person at the organization? Looking from the perspective of the donor's self-interest, by whom would they be most flattered to be asked? To whom could this person only say yes?

Keep putting yourself in the donor's shoes. Will they feel receptive to being asked now?

3. *Exactly what will be asked for?*
Will you be asking this person for a single Leadership or Challenge Gift to be announced at your Benevon Free One-Hour Ask Event to inspire additional giving, or will their gift be combined with others for a pooled Challenge Gift?

4. *Where will the Ask take place?*
The best place to ask is the place that is closest to the emotional appeal of your work. For an arboretum, you might ask outside while walking through the park; for a children's museum you could ask at the museum café, within earshot of happy, playful children.

5. *What is the bottom-line result you will come away with?*
It is good to have a range of Asks, starting with the biggest, then scaling back to the bottom line. It is often helpful to ask for other types of contributions (in addition to the money you will be asking for), such as serving as an Ambassador or hosting a Free Feel-Good Cultivation Event.

6. *What makes you think this person is ready to be asked now?*
Have there been any recent cues? Have you hinted to the donor that you will be asking for their support soon? Has the donor asked you what you need? Keep putting yourself in the donor's shoes. Will they feel receptive to being asked now?

Donors want to say yes. Don't embarrass them by asking for something that, from their perspective, they barely have enough of.

7. *What are your biggest concerns, fears, and reasons for procrastinating in making this Ask?*
   Don't be reluctant to list even seemingly trivial things. Often these are legitimate, especially if they pertain to donor readiness.

8. *Does the person have an abundance of what you are asking for?*
   If you don't know or are unsure, how could you find out? Who could you ask? Donors want to say yes. Don't embarrass them by asking for something that, from their perspective, they barely have enough of. You may need to do more homework to find out.

9. *What is the person's self-interest in saying yes?*
   How good would they feel saying yes? How sorry will they feel saying no? Is there enough positive self-interest? Ultimately, their emotional connection to your mission is what will sustain them as a lifelong donor.

10. *What concerns might this person have about saying yes to your request?*
    Again, put yourself in the donor's shoes. Add in your worst fears. Things like: the donor is still offended that we thanked him too late for his last gift; the donor doesn't like the direction our new program has taken; the donor's true allegiance was to our former director—he doesn't like our new director as well. These will be important for you to know so you can address them in the cultivation process and not wait to address them in the Ask.

Donors will never bring up recognition. You must weave it into the Ask.

11. *What might strengthen this Ask?*
    What could you add to the Ask that would make it nearly impossible for the person to say no: a different asker, an additional asker, a memorial gift, a Leadership or Challenge Gift, more years to spread out the payment, or a particular type of recognition?

12. *How would this person most like to be recognized?*
    Donors will never bring up recognition. You must weave it into the Ask. Let them know how "all donors at this level" will be recognized—at special receptions with the scholarship recipients, meetings with important speakers, dinners at elegant homes, and so on. Try to give them two or three options for special recognition that fit with their preferences, which you should know by the time you make the Ask, especially if their gift will be a Leadership Gift.

13. *How can this person invite others to participate?*
    Once they have said yes, their natural tendency will be to want to share their enthusiasm for this organization with others—it's good to mention some of those opportunities during the Ask.

14. *What would be possible for your organization if the person says yes?*
    Spend some time thinking through your response to this question, not only what it would mean for your programs and services, but what it could mean for the donor: perhaps she would like to be asked to join your board. Think about the donor's Treasure Map. Who else might they naturally want to involve or invite to a Point of Entry?

15. *What other questions are still unanswered?*
    If you have answered all of the questions above thoroughly, you have probably uncovered some new ones. Remember, the more prepared you feel going into the Ask, the better.

Practice Asking for a Leadership or Challenge Gift

Once you are able to answer each question in the list confidently, your donor is ready to be asked.

Here is an outline of the script for asking for a Leadership or Challenge Gift.

SCRIPT FOR ASKING FOR A LEADERSHIP OR CHALLENGE GIFT

I. Thank you for being with us today.

II. [Acknowledge their past support, as specifically as possible, including examples of what their prior gifts have allowed you to do (e.g., serve ___ more kids, expand the art program, conduct ___ more research studies on the path to finding the cure).]

III. [Mention the emotional connection to their favorite aspect of your work (e.g., say, "Sally wanted me to say thank you on behalf of the pediatric AIDS program—we are seeing such great results in the kids who are fortunate enough to be in the program").]

IV. Today we want to talk with you about something new, something very special. As you know, we are working systematically to grow our base of donors who really believe in our work. That's why we have the __________ [your POE] and the __________ [your Ask Event].

    Our goal is to raise $______ at our next event. And, to help us do that, we would like to be able to announce a special (leadership/ challenge) gift of $_____ at the event, to inspire additional giving. These funds would enable us to ______________.

    We are coming to you today to ask you to be a part of this special gift by making a contribution of $______________.

(Be prepared with two questions to ask, things you really would like their input on.)

continued on page 173

continued from page 172

SCRIPT FOR ASKING FOR A LEADERSHIP OR CHALLENGE GIFT

V. Possible questions and responses:

If They Ask	Tell Them
1. Who else will you be asking?	The other names or at least the names of some of the other people they might recognize.
2. How does this pooled gift concept work?	The total pool will go towards your ____society, which funds x, y, and z (your three buckets), and emphasize their specific area of interest with a fact (like the number of people you still have to turn away every day in that program area), a need (e.g. for more tutors or after school programs) and a story of a life that could be changed or has been changed in that program.
3. What will the money be used for?	It goes to support all the work of your program, the areas of greatest need, such as (your three giving levels or the programs they fund).
4. How would you want me to pay it (all at once, over several years)?	They can pay it annually over five years or sooner if they prefer.
5. How does my former pledge fit into this?	This would be in addition to their existing pledge.
6. Do I need to come to the breakfast/lunch?	Only if they would like to. Invite them to sit at a VIP table or to be a Table Captain.

Role Play Each Ask

We spend a lot of time in our workshops role playing Asks and the thing we hear over and over again is how valuable the practice is for people. Even though the real Ask will no doubt be different when you do it, practicing helps you work through and anticipate many of the donor's concerns and discover in advance which donors you may not be ready to ask yet.

The process of asking is fun and natural. The biggest challenge is to remember that it needs to be a dialog between two people who already know each other.

As you practice asking in a role-play situation prior to the real Ask, do not default to thinking you are asking a complete stranger. Likewise, if you are playing the role of donor, do not pretend you hardly know this group and that they are bothering you. Neither is true. This is a relationship. You know one another well by now. The donor knows in advance that in this meeting they will be asked for money. In fact, they are looking forward to saying yes!

It bears repeating that if you are hesitating to ask, trust your instincts. If you have even the slightest sense that asking this person for money would be awkward or premature, then hold off asking until you have had another cultivation contact. The last thing you would want is to have this donor be upset with you, after all the time you have taken to cultivate this relationship.

You should practice asking—at least two times for each donor—before you make the real Ask. It's fine to practice with the other people in your organization who may know these donors or the situation. You can even practice with a "stranger." Tell them some of your biggest fears so they can be sure to play on them during the practice session.

Briefing for the role-play: Brief the person you will be "asking" by answering these questions:

- What is this donor's past giving history with your organization?
- What are two or three concerns this donor might have about giving to you?
- Where will the Ask take place?
- What are your biggest fears in asking this person?

Making the Ask

The process of asking is fun and natural. The biggest challenge is to remember that it needs to be a dialog between two people who already know each other.

Before I go to ask someone for money, I always put myself in the donor's shoes.

Before I go to ask someone for money, I always put myself in the donor's shoes. How would I like to be approached by one or two key people from the organization, knowing full well what they want from me? I recall that this is an organization I love and will feel excited to support. It feels as though I have guided myself through the cultivation process. In fact, the process has felt very natural. I am wondering why no one has asked me to give until now. I have given many readiness signs to this group, hosted an event in my home, and invited friends to Point of Entry Events. This is one of the two or three places I want to give my money. I love these people and support what they are up to.

To provide some encouragement for what may lie ahead as you enter the cultivation and asking process, let me share two heartwarming Ask stories from our alumni groups. One group had a lunchtime major Ask for $1 million scheduled with the executive director, the board chair (who was also a major donor), and a well-cultivated donor, but on the day of the appointment, the donor had to cancel. Rather than postponing the meeting, the donor called that morning to apologize, insisting on knowing how much money the organization needed. Despite the executive director's attempts to hem and haw and reschedule the lunch so the Ask could take place in person, the donor persisted and the nervous executive director finally blurted out, "We were planning to ask you to give $1 million towards the capital campaign for our new building." The donor replied, "I'd be delighted to do that—just send me all the paperwork."

The moral of that story is to never underestimate the power of the highly personal donor-cultivation work you will be doing. This same executive director, who has now raised over $10 million for this campaign, calls me often with amazing success stories and to ask me, "How can we attract and cultivate more of these wonderful donors who truly understand and appreciate our work?"

At this point, asking should be nothing more than nudging the inevitable.

"Do it for Us, Bob!"

But let's suppose you aren't getting millions of dollars over the phone. Let's assume you'll need to go out and meet with people to ask. What else does it take to be successful when you ask?

We worked with one very shy executive director of a children's home who, even after many cultivation visits and practice Asks, could barely bring himself to make the Ask for $100,000. His 27-year tenure with the organization was a testament to his love of the children and the work of the organization. We suggested that when he goes out to make the Ask, rather than nervously anticipating all the ways things could go wrong, he should pause to recall his larger purpose. "Imagine the little kids, tugging at your pant legs as you walk out of the office, saying, "Do it for us, Bob! You can do it! We need the things the money will buy."

He became a fearless, highly successful asker after that, and yes, he secured that $100,000 gift—for the kids!

Be Authentic

Once you have completed your preparation and practice Asks, you need to put it all aside. At this point, asking should be nothing more than nudging the inevitable. You are asking people who already know and love your organization. You already know they have what you are asking for. You already know they are emotionally connected to you.

I recommend you go into the Ask with an entirely different agenda: in those few minutes, see how related and connected you can become with the donor. It is all about listening for every cue and being much more focused on what they are saying right now than on what you should say next.

The key to a successful Ask is you being a real human being—not a robot with a script, but a regular person who truly cares about this organization and this donor. The more

You want each donor to feel as though they have sprinkled fairy dust on the most worthy organization in the world.

authentic you can be, the better. Asking someone for money is an intimate occasion. It can be serious, playful, short and to-the-point, or long and drawn-out. No two Asks are ever the same, because no two people are the same. I recommend you approach it more like your first dance with your new, lifelong dance partner. You may step on each other's toes, grumble and laugh a bit, but eventually you will get it right. As with dancing, one person is the leader. In asking for money, it should go without saying that the donor is the leader.

Even after doing all your cultivation, some donors may say no to part or all of what you ask for. Your job if they do say no is to thank them for being a friend of your organization and to ask if there are any other ways they would like to be involved. Then your job is to figure out how to ask them again in exactly the way they want to be asked, for exactly the thing they do want to say yes to. And then you ask them again, or have the perfect person ask them, so they say yes and feel great about it.

If they say yes and don't feel great about it, it's not a "win." You don't want to leave them with any sense of having been manipulated into giving more than they were comfortable giving. You don't need their contribution that badly. You want each donor to feel as though they have sprinkled fairy dust on the most worthy organization in the world. You want each donor to feel so good about giving to you that they have no need for others to even know they did it. You want them to feel as if supporting your organization is a source of personal pleasure for them.

You have to let them know how excited you are to receive their gifts. You cannot be just a little bit appreciative. Let them know right away that their gifts are a big deal to you. Then you will have made a real friend. You have allowed them to truly contribute and feel the way you feel when you know you have made a real contribution.

Rather than giving out of guilt or obligation to a friend who is on your board, these donors have chosen to become—and remain—involved with you, for their own reasons.

Cultivating lifelong donors and connecting them to your work is the real nugget of the Benevon Model. Once established and nurtured, that personal connection becomes the driver of the relationship. Rather than giving out of guilt or obligation to a friend who is on your board, these donors have chosen to become—and remain—involved with you, for their own reasons. Multiply that by hundreds, even thousands of donors, and you can begin to see over the horizon to long-term sustainability for your organization.

Sponsorships

One final way to maximize your event results is to have your event sponsored by one or two companies that already support your work. This adds credibility and lets every dollar given go right to the bottom line. Your organization determines the desired dollar amount of the sponsorship. At a minimum, it should cover the costs of putting on the event.

As your event grows in stature each year, you may be able to raise the price of the sponsorship and offer more visibility for the corporation than they would have received for sponsoring your golf tournament or other smaller special event.

I would caution against having too many sponsors, for fear the event will quickly be perceived as a traditional fundraising event where corporate sponsors "buy" tables and the guests are invited by the sponsor, usually having no prior knowledge or interest in the organization's work.

Ideally, each of your sponsors will be from a company whose leaders really understand and appreciate your mission. Perhaps they have been well cultivated and involved as volunteers or beneficiaries of your work. Perhaps they have been serving as Ambassadors.

One group serving people with intellectual disabilities has as their Ask Event sponsor a company that employs several of their consumers.

As with asking for a Leadership or Challenge Gift, by the time you ask for the Sponsorship Gift, you will know the bucket area of greatest impact to the sponsor. Be sure to practice asking for the Sponsorship Gift, including good examples of what the gift will allow your organization to provide in that particular area, for example, serving 300 more children, cleaning up four more hiking trails, etc.

As you thank your sponsors for their generous gifts, consider inviting them to participate in the Ask Event as a Table Captain or testimonial speaker, but only if they have been directly involved with your organization. One group serving people with intellectual disabilities has as their Ask Event sponsor a company that employs several of their consumers. That sponsor also did a brilliant job as a testimonial speaker, sharing all he had learned and gained personally from working with the organization.

Having a Leadership or Challenge Gift and a Sponsorship Gift are essential to getting it right at your first Ask Event.

CHAPTER 14

STEP ELEVEN: PLANNING YOUR ASK EVENT

In this chapter, we will define the Benevon Free One-Hour Ask Event, clarify its objectives, and make your Ask Event Plan, including your financial projections.

The Benevon Free One-Hour Ask Event Defined

The Benevon Free One-Hour Ask Event is distinct from all other events. If you have come this far in learning how the Benevon Model works, you are no doubt committed to getting it right. I encourage you, if you want to be successful in putting on this event, to put aside—even temporarily—all the other events you may think it resembles and just learn how this event works. Like everything else in the Benevon Model, it follows a particular format that has been designed based on tested metrics and formulas.

The ultimate objective of the Benevon Ask Event is to "harvest" new Point of Entry guests each year, having at least 10% of them join your Multiple-Year Giving Society. So an Ask Event with 100 guests would have at least 10 guests who pledge to give $1,000 or more annually for five years.

Keep your Ask Events small and focus on the key metrics. Your objective is to grow this pool of donors whom you will cultivate personally over time for further volunteer involvement: as Ambassadors, committee members, and board

The best part about it, besides the bottom line, of course, is that the entire hour is spent educating and inspiring the audience about your work.

members, as well as for larger major gifts, capital, and endowment.

Guests are invited to the Ask Event word-of-mouth by a Table Captain, ideally a friend or colleague who also served as an Ambassador in the months leading up to the Ask Event. Each guest is told that the event is free to attend, it will last no longer than 60 minutes, breakfast or lunch will be served, and they will be asked to give money at the end of the hour. However, there is no minimum and no maximum gift expected. In other words, it is fine for them to give nothing at all.

The Free One-Hour Ask Event has a particular format; there is *nothing* haphazard about it. The program elements are sequenced so as to build to a crescendo at the end of the hour. At that point, the guests have been sufficiently educated and inspired, in such a natural and respectful manner, that they are able to choose freely whether or not they would like to contribute financially by becoming a part of your organization's Multiple-Year Giving Society.

Far from being a high-pressure, obligatory giving event, the Benevon Free One-Hour Ask Event provides people with an unforgettable, succinct presentation of the extraordinary work of your organization. Whether or not your guests choose to make a financial contribution at the event, they will be thanking you for having invited them.

Compared to the events most nonprofits are now busy producing, this type of event requires significantly less work. The best part about it, besides the bottom line, of course, is that the entire hour is spent educating and inspiring the audience about your work.

Projecting Your Ask Event Results

To understand Benevon's Ask Event Results Formula, let's walk through the plan that Abilities in Action makes to project their results from their first Free One-Hour Ask Event.

FREE ONE HOUR ASK EVENT PLAN

1. Name of organization: Abilities in Action
2. Date of Ask Event: May 15
3. Venue: Nice Hotel
4. Number of guests: 200
5. Minimum number of Ask Event guests who must have attended a Point of Entry in the prior year (40% of #4 above): 80
6. Total starting number of Table Captains required: 28

Gifts	Formula		Stretch	
	Donors/ Cash & Pledges (# / $)	Cash Only	Donors/ Cash & Pledges (# / $)	Cash Only
$1K x 5 years	20 / 100K	20K	20 / 100K	20K
$5K x 5 years	0 / 0	0	2 / 50K	10K
$10K x 5 years	0 / 0	0	0 / 0	0
Subtotal	20 / 100K	20K	22 / 150K	30K
Sponsor $	10K	10K	10K	10K
Leadership/ Challenge $	25K	5K	35K	20K
Total	135K	35K	195K	60K

Starting at the top: Abilities in Action has to make some key decisions right off the bat, deciding the date of their Ask Event, the venue, and the number of guest in attendance.

An inexpensive breakfast or lunch is free of the "baggage" associated with dinner events and gives guests the freedom to choose either to give to your mission or not to give at all.

Date

The best times of the year for an Ask Event are spring (April, May, June) or fall (October, November, and early December). The only exception we make is for communities with many seasonal residents. If your organization is located in such a community, you will want to plan your event for a month when those seasonal residents are there. Because of the lead time in preparing for the Ask Event—recruiting Table Captains, putting on the requisite number of Point of Entry Events, and making the necessary Follow-Up Calls—April is often the best month for "snowbird" communities, for example.

As to best days of the week and best times of day to schedule the first event, we recommend Tuesday, Wednesday, or Thursday, for breakfast or lunch. The Ask Event may not take place in the evening—no cocktail hours, dinners, or dessert buffets. This needs to be a daytime event. Evening events come with their own unwritten ground rules—generally a ticket price for admission, plus the expectation of spending additional money on tangible goods or services. If they are asked to give at a dinner event, people tend to give just enough to cover the cost of the dinner. An inexpensive breakfast or lunch is free of the "baggage" associated with dinner events and gives guests the freedom to choose either to give to your mission or not to give at all.

To decide between breakfast or lunch, consider the time that would work best for most of your guests. Working people tend to prefer an early breakfast that they can drive to before they start their work day. Those who have a little more flexibility in their schedules may prefer lunch. You will never please everyone; aim to please the majority. The location of the event may also influence the time of day that you choose. How accessible is this location to the freeway? Is there good parking? Is it easy to find? Will people be able to get in and out quickly?

We require the groups we train and coach to have between 200 and 300 people at each year's Ask Event.

Venue

After you have decided when to hold the event, you can zero in on your ideal venue. Many groups deliberate over whether or not to have their event at an upscale hotel versus right in their own lunchroom or meeting space. I generally recommend going upscale for the Ask Event. It sends out a message that you are legitimate, professional, and here to stay. Save your office or program venue for your Point of Entry Events. In smaller, rural communities, we recommend having the Ask Event in the best wedding venue in town.

Your next concern in booking your venue should be price. To determine that, start with your biggest budget item: food. All the food should be cold and pre-set when the guests arrive. You do not want to have serving people distracting your guests during those precious 60 minutes when you will want their undivided attention. Besides the food, the only other budget item you may have difficulty getting donated is the cost of the audio/visual services on the day of the event. You will need a sound system and the equipment to project your video professionally. This can be pricey. We recommend budgeting $20 to $25 per person, all told, to cover the cost of each Ask Event. Note that this does not include the cost of producing your seven-minute video, which many groups are able to have donated to them.

Number of Guests

Early on, you will need to decide how big an event you will have, since your financial projections will be based, largely, on that number. We require the groups we train and coach to have between 200 and 300 people at each year's Ask Event. Having tested many different sizes for Ask Events over the years, we have arrived at this size after careful consideration.

Given the amount of work needed to put on the event, fixed costs (such as video production), and the fact that you will need a new 40% of "ripened fruit" guests each year, 200

Do not aim to grow the size of your event every year.

guests seems to be a stable minimum number, even in smaller communities. Any larger than 300 guests has groups inviting too many new people and using the Ask Event as a substitute for a Point of Entry Event. Staff becomes consumed with party planning rather than Point of Entry work.

Beware of succumbing to the illusion of having the "best fundraising event in town," which usually means people just had a great time at your party. It does not necessarily correlate to dollars raised or guests' experience of the mission. *Do not aim to grow the size of your event every year.* Prior years' happy donors may come back as Table Captains, ideally having served as Ambassadors in the ensuing year. Many of your prior guests will be invited to your Free Feel-Good Cultivation Events and some you will "bless-and-release" entirely.

Ripened Fruit: 40% Minimum

For their 200-person Ask Event, Abilities in Action calculates that 80% of those 200 guests will have attended a Point of Entry Event before their Ask Event.

Starting Number of Table Captains

DETERMINING THE NUMBER OF TABLE CAPTAINS YOU NEED

Number of Ask Event guests in attendance:	Number of Table Captains you need to start with:
200	28
250	35
300	43

Our statistics for determining the number of Table Captains you need to recruit are built into the numbers in the chart above.

Far better to project realistically using these proven formulas than to have empty seats and pay for uneaten meals.

Note that in order to end up with 20 Table Captains for a 200-guest Ask event, you will need to start with 28. Why? First, assume that at least 15% of the people who initially agree to be Table Captains will not actually end up being Table Captains on the day of your Ask Event. They are not bad people; they meant well when they accepted the assignment, but for whatever reason, they were unable to deliver. Do not be surprised on event day. Plan for this 15% Table Captain attrition, which takes the 28 Table Captains down to 23.

Second, you must assume that, even for the Table Captains who do come through, at least 15% of their guests will not attend. Although the Table Captains will have made two check-in calls to each invited guest in the week before the event, on the day of the event, for one reason or another—a sick child, a medical emergency, or the weather—those 15% will be unable to attend. Factor this percentage into your numbers. It takes you down three more, to 20 Table Captains.

Twenty-eight Table Captains is quite a lot more than the 20 Table Captains you might have planned for without this chart. Far better to project realistically using these proven formulas than to have empty seats and pay for uneaten meals.

Choosing Your Three Giving Levels

Moving to the next part of the Ask Event Plan on page 183, Abilities in Action has to choose their three giving levels, or Units of Service. Because they have not received a gift of $10,000 or more in the past two years, they select Option 1: $1,000, $5,000, and $10,000 a year for five years, following our formula.

Setting Your Goals: Money Raised and Number of Guests

When it comes to setting your financial goal for the event, the gross amount raised at the Ask Event is a direct function

... the only true test of an outstanding Ask Event is whether or not 10% of the guests join the Multiple-Year Giving Society at $1,000 or more for five years.

of the number of people in attendance. The average group we train and coach through the process raises $200,000 at their first Benevon Ask Event in cash and pledges.

If you are planning to implement the Benevon Model on your own, I would recommend that you reduce these projections by 50% or more. While you may do better than this at your first Ask Event, there are so many questions that will come up along the way, the answers to which will be counterintuitive, that you should plan to make some mistakes and factor that into your bottom line right from the start.

Benevon's Two Key Ask Event Metrics

We use two key metrics that work together to project your Ask Event's success.

First, our overall formula for a successful Ask Event: take the number of people who attend the Ask Event and divide that number by two. Then multiply the remaining number by $1,000 to determine how much money your event should raise. In other words, assuming 40% "newly ripened fruit," an event with 200 people in attendance should raise at least $100,000 in cash *and pledges*.

Second, regardless of the number of attendees, the overall metric you should be striving for is to have a minimum of 10% of your Ask Event guests join your Multiple-Year Giving Society each year. Far more than having a higher percentage of total givers at your Ask Event, the only true test of an outstanding Ask Event is whether or not 10% of the guests join the Multiple-Year Giving Society at $1,000 or more for five years.

A related metric, about which we are equally strict, and one that surprises many people, is that we only want to see about half (40% to 50%) of Ask Event guests making any financial gift at all at the event. Recall the 40% ripened-fruit percentage (Chapter 3). These are the guests your Ask Event is aiming to convert to Multiple-Year Donors. For everyone else,

If your event is yielding more than half of the guests giving money, you have deviated from the process in some way.

your event will serve as a good Pre-Point of Entry and therefore we would not want most of these people to give money yet, because they have not been properly engaged and cultivated. If your event is yielding more than half of the guests giving money, you have deviated from the process in some way.

Back to Abilities in Action, who are planning a 200-person Ask Event. They must plan their budget for the worst case, the "Formula" column. According to our metrics, that would be $100,000 in cash and pledges in the subtotal box before adding in the Leadership/Challenge Gift and Sponsorship.

To decide how to spread this $100,000 out across their three giving levels, they work backwards from the goal. They project, according to our formula, that 10% of the guests will join the Multiple-Year Giving Society. Ten percent of 200 people is 20 guests that would each join at at least the lowest level of $1,000 a year for five years, which adds up to $100,000 in pledges at this event. In order to apply the 10% rule, their projections do not need to be based on any higher than the lowest of the three levels.

Notice the column in the Formula section of the Ask Event Plan, listing "Cash Only" raised. To be conservative, Abilities in Action assumes that their Leadership Gift will come from several donors and total $25,000, of which only $5,000 will be cash. The remaining $20,000 they project will be in the form of future pledges. They also project Sponsorship Gifts totaling $10,000, which will all be in current cash, no pledges. Adding these figures ($25,000 and $10,000) to the $100,000 in cash and five-year pledges meant they budget to raise $135,000 from this event.

While the total dollars committed at the event, including pledges, would be $135,000, the cash raised on the day of the event would be only $35,000. This is important to notice and to alert the board to this fact in advance of the event.

Abilities in Action's financial projections for this event meet both of our key Ask Event metrics.

Note that there is no objective or metric to grow the size of your Ask Event year after year. On the contrary, the event must stay small and manageable so as to focus on the primary objective of the Ask Event: inviting the prior year's Point of Entry guests to join the Multiple-Year Giving Society.

Cumulative Value of Multiple-Year Pledges

While the day-of-event cash may not be as impressive as you would like, the payoff rate on the five-year pledges should be over 95%. That is because you do not merely invoice donors for each of the next five years and then wait to invite them back to the Ask Event in the sixth year. Rather, you begin the deeper cultivation process on the day after the first Ask Event they attend. Their multiple-year pledge at one of your higher giving levels needs to be regarded as the donor's way of telling you they truly believe in your work and want to stay connected to you, perhaps becoming even more involved. Without this ongoing, personalized cultivation, you will not achieve a 95% payoff rate.

This chart illustrates the impact of the Multiple-Year pledges. Imagine waking up on January 1 of your organization's fifth year of implementing the model, knowing the cumulative effect of those pledges.

THE CUMULATIVE VALUE OF MULTIPLE-YEAR PLEDGES

	YEAR 1	YEAR 2	YEAR 3	YEAR 4	YEAR 5
$100K					Year 5 Pledges
$80K				Year 4 Pledges	Year 4 Pledges
$60K			Year 3 Pledges	Year 3 Pledges	Year 3 Pledges
$40K		Year 2 Pledges	Year 2 Pledges	Year 2 Pledges	Year 2 Pledges
$20K	Year 1 Pledges	Year 1 Pledges	Year 1 Pledges	Year 1 Pledges	Year 1 Pledges

The key point to take away from this discussion of Ask Event results is that the only way you will attain these desired metrics is if you have at least 40% newly ripened fruit at each Ask Event.

Stretch Goal

Now you can have fun filling in the right side of the Ask Event Plan with whatever bigger goals you'd like to achieve. We call this the "stretch" column. You can see that Abilities in Action added two donors at their middle giving level, $5,000 for five years. And they increased their Leadership/ Challenge Gift as well as the percentage of it that would be paid in cash versus pledges. You can see how quickly their bottom line increased from $135,000 to $195,000. And their "cash only" went from $35,000 to $60,000.

What About One-Time Gifts?

People often ask why we do not include any gifts of lower amounts in the financial projections. That is because we are not focusing on one-year-at-a-time gifts to build sustainable funding. The focus is on five-year pledges of $1,000 or more. A successful Ask Event will have no more than 50% of the guests making a financial contribution that day. The other 50% or more may choose to come to a true Point of Entry Event after the Ask Event to learn more, to talk with someone else before making their gift, or not to give at all. In other words, the event organizers need to be counting on a maximum of only half the people making a gift at the event, including those who make smaller gifts. Take note if you have more than 50% of the Ask Event guests making a gift at your event. This generally indicates too little ripened fruit or too much pressure in the pitch.

Results Takeaway

The key point to take away from this discussion of Ask Event results is that the only way you will attain these desired metrics is if you have at least 40% newly ripened fruit at each Ask Event. And the only way you will have that is if you focus on having sizzling Point of Entry Events that your Ambassadors and guests will want to invite others to attend.

Using your Ask Event as a Point of Entry Event is not sustainable.

So it all comes back to the Point of Entry. The Point of Entry drives the model. The Ask Event is the third step in the Benevon Model, not the first step; it is not designed to do the heavy lifting of the Point of Entry Event.

Using your Ask Event as a Point of Entry Event is not sustainable. I certainly do not recommend trying the Ask Event—*even one time*—if you have not done the proper Point of Entry work leading up to it.

Summary: Ask Event Rules

We refer to these Ask Event rules as "the non-negotiables" because we have tested them with teams from over 4,000 nonprofit organizations. Although you may not like them or you may feel certain they are wrong, if you are committed to getting the Benevon Model right, I urge you to follow them. These rules work.

1. The Ask Event must be free for all guests to attend. Free is magical. The free event allows people the freedom to choose whether or not to give, and, as a result, those who do choose to give will give more generously.

2. The Ask Event must be a one-hour breakfast or a lunch event, taking place on a weekday. All food is cold and pre-set before the guests arrive. Carafes of hot coffee and tea are placed on the table in advance. There are no serving people bustling around the room, clearing plates, and distracting guests from your all-important program.

Your Ask Event size must be 200 to 300 people, not smaller, not bigger.

3. The event must last for 60 minutes at the longest. No matter what, you must start on time. Even if only 40% or 50% of the people are in the room by then, start on time. Plan the timeline for your program to last for 50 minutes to allow yourself a cushion. Aim to finish early. Rehearse your program as many times as necessary with the actual participants until you are certain you can do it all in 50 to 60 minutes. Have a timekeeper seated prominently at one of the front tables to cue your speakers if they are running out of time. Tell your speakers in advance where the timekeeper will be sitting and how they will signal speakers to end on time.

4. Your Ask Event size must be 200 to 300 people, not smaller, not bigger. Use the Ask Event solely for the purpose it is intended: to add new donors to your Multiple-Year Giving Society each year.

   Again, do not start smaller than 200 people. You will be disappointed in your bottom-line results when compared with all the work you put into this. Two hundred guests is the minimum size to make this all worthwhile.

   Do not grow your Ask Event larger than 300 guests. Resist the temptation to have this event become the most popular event in town. Do not use your Ask Event as a Free Feel-Good Cultivation Event (Point of Re-Entry Event) where you gather your major donors every year to remind them of your great work. Instead, spend the rest of your time deepening your organization's relationship with your new Multiple-Year Giving Society Donors via one-on-one cultivation visits and small Free Feel-Good Cultivation Events focused on their particular bucket area of interest.

You must keep watering the tree if you expect to have newly ripened fruit to pick each year.

5. Ask Event Key Metric #1: At least 40% of your Ask Event guests must have attended a Point of Entry Event in the year prior to this Ask Event—the "ripened fruit" percentage. In order to meet this formula, year after year, you will need a robust, self-refreshing Ambassador program that generates two Point of Entry Events per month, each with 10 to 15 people in attendance.

   Do not use your Ask Event as a substitute for a Point of Entry Event. You will rapidly run out of guests or leave your guests thinking your Ask Event is a traditional, old-reality fundraising event. That is not sustainable. You must keep watering the tree if you expect to have newly ripened fruit to pick each year.

6. Ask Event Key Metric #2: The ultimate measure of a successful Ask Event is having a minimum of 10% of the guests join your Multiple-Year Giving Society at one of your three major giving levels. This one metric gauges the internal integrity of your organization's entire implementation of the Benevon Model.

7. Your Multiple-Year Giving Society must have three (and only three) giving levels. These are your Units of Service. There are two options for these levels, which are determined based on past giving history in your organization. Once established, these levels never change.
   - Option 1: $1,000, $5,000, and $10,000 a year for five years
   - Option 2: $1,000, $10,000, and $25,000 a year for five years

To repeat: you may not have more than three Units of Service.

Note that the lowest level in both options is $1,000 a year for five years. A donor who gives anything over that amount—and pledges to continue to give that amount for five years—is considered to be a member of your Multiple-Year Giving Society, even if they do not give at exactly one of your three giving levels. For example, a donor who pledges to give $2,500 a year for five years is definitely a member of your giving society.

To determine which of the two giving-level options to use, answer this questions: in the past two years, is the largest gift your organization has received from one individual been $10,000 or higher? If not, then you must use the three giving levels in Option 1 above. If so, then your three giving levels must be those in Option 2 above.

To repeat: you may not have more than three Units of Service.

8. Using the two key metrics (rules #5 and #6 above), budget your event to attain Benevon's Ask Event Results Formula, nothing more: take the number of people who attend the Ask Event and divide that number by two. Then multiply the remaining number by $1,000 to determine how much money your event should raise. In other words, assuming 40% newly ripened fruit, an event with 200 people in attendance should raise at least $100,000 in cash *and pledges*. Since you will be doing this on your own, without the help of Benevon's trained coaches, I would suggest that you budget conservatively for half of our standard formula amount, which in this case would be $50,000 in cash and pledges.

In other words, the Ask Event may not be used to ask for capital, restricted giving for special projects, or endowment.

9. Be thoughtful in naming your Multiple-Year Giving Society and your three Units of Service (recalling the name examples in Chapter 8). Be sure they make sense when put together. For example, a camp calls their giving society the Sponsor-a-Camper Society and their levels are named Sponsor a Camper, Sponsor a Cabin, and Sponsor a Camp. Once you name your giving society and choose your levels, these never change.

10. Make Follow-Up Calls to all Table Captains and Multiple-Year Donors the day after the Ask Event. You do not need to call every guest who attended the event. Follow the guidelines in Chapter 15.

11. All of the funds raised at the Ask Event, even after you have been having this Ask Event for many years, must be unrestricted so they can be used for the general operating needs of the organization. In other words, the Ask Event may not be used to ask for capital, restricted giving for special projects, or endowment. For those major donors who may wish to give to your capital or endowment programs, their gift to your Multiple-Year Giving Society remains their basic unrestricted gift each year. Their capital or endowment gifts are in addition to this annual pledge.

Now that you are armed with your thoughtful plan, let's move on to producing your successful Ask Event.

CHAPTER 15:

STEP TWELVE: PRODUCING A SUCCESSFUL ASK EVENT

You've worked so hard to get to this point. Let's look at some of the keys to ensuring that your first Ask Event is successful, starting with what it will take to have every seat filled with someone who will be ready to give when asked.

To recap, your organization has been putting on two Point of Entry Events per month for the past 9 to 12 months. At least half of your Point of Entry guests were invited to attend their Point of Entry by an Ambassador. The remaining guests were invited by board members, friends of the organization, or staff who did not become official Ambassadors.

Your warm and engaging staff member followed up diligently with each Point of Entry guest, blessing-and-releasing at least 50% of those guests. The remaining 50%—those who were not blessed-and-released—are the group of people you want to have attend your Ask Event. For purposes of this discussion, we consider them to be "ripened fruit," as defined in Chapter 3.

How will you invite them to attend? There are two ways—what we refer to as the primary and secondary invitation strategies.

You should expect, realistically, that only four or five people at each Ask Event table will be ripened fruit—since you will have blessed-and-released half the Point of Entry guests.

Primary Invitation Strategy

The primary invitation strategy begins three months before your Ask Event when you invite each of your successful Ambassadors to become Table Captains. For most Ambassadors, this will be a natural and welcome role. These are your strongest champions. They were your gold-standard Ambassadors from the beginning or they became Ambassadors during the follow-up process after attending your Point of Entry Event. They have had at least 10 guests attend a private Point of Entry Event or one of your regularly scheduled public Points of Entry. They have witnessed the enthusiasm of their Point of Entry guests, many of whom may have been asking them, "When are they going to ask me for money?" These Ambassadors will be delighted to serve as Table Captains and fill their tables of 10 with their well cultivated guests.

You should expect, realistically, that only four or five people at each Ask Event table will be ripened fruit—since you will have blessed-and-released half the Point of Entry guests. Therefore those Ambassadors who agree to become Table Captains will also be expected to fill the rest of their table of 10 with five or six new people who may not yet have attended a Point of Entry.

This strategy assures that all remaining "unattached" Point of Entry guests who have not been blessed-and-released will be invited to the Ask Event.

Secondary Invitation Strategy

The Secondary Invitation Strategy also begins three months before the Ask Event. This strategy assures that all remaining "unattached" Point of Entry guests who have not been blessed-and-released will be invited to the Ask Event. After all your hard work to bring these people through Points of Entry, follow up with and cultivate them, you certainly don't want to overlook inviting every single person who has not been blessed-and-released to the Ask Event.

These remaining unattached Point of Entry guests fall into one of two categories:

- First are the Point of Entry guests whose Ambassador declined to become a Table Captain. You should plan for this to happen. Some decline because they are too busy, others decline because they don't like events or they just do not want to be responsible for filling a table of 10 people. That is fine. You will ask these Ambassadors for their permission to invite their Point of Entry guests to the Ask Event and seat them with other people who have agreed to become Table Captains. Since your organization has now developed a relationship of its own with these Point of Entry guests, they will be likely to say yes when you call to invite them to sit at the table of another person they may know or a VIP table hosted by one of your board members who has not served as an Ambassador this year. Here is the script we use for converting an Ambassador to a Table Captain.

SCRIPT FOR CONVERTING AMBASSADORS TO TABLE CAPTAINS
BENEVON FREE ONE-HOUR ASK EVENT

You have been a good friend and Ambassador to our organization and a real supporter of our mission. You have invited many people to attend our one-hour tours. I'd like to invite you to consider participating in a new way with us—by being a Table Captain at our upcoming fundraising breakfast.

This event is different from other events we have done in the past.

- The goal of the event is to raise unrestricted funds for our programs and to spread our message in the community.
- It's totally free.
- It will only be an hour long.
- There is no requirement that anyone give money at the event.
- It will be our job to inspire people so that they will want to give.
- As much as anything, we want people to come and find out about the great work we do.
- It will make you proud to be involved with us.

Each Table Captain is asked to fill a table of 10 people by inviting them personally. Invite the friends, co-workers, family, neighbors who have already attended our __________ (Point of Entry) tours. Your job is to get them to attend. You do not have to ask anyone for money.

Here are the details (date and time) of the event.

Would you help us by being a Table Captain for our event?

If yes: Great! Thanks! We'll have (name of person) call and meet with you to go over all the details. We'll also have reminder cards for you to give to people you invite. Remember, we have several __________ (Point of Entry Events) scheduled for additional people to come and learn about us before the event .

Please make sure you invite and confirm enough people for the table to be filled. Expect 2-4 people to cancel on the day of the event, so we recommend confirming 12-14 people, to make sure 10 will be there.

Thanks again! You will have a great time, and you'll be very proud of us!

If maybe or need to consider: When will you know? Is there any more information you need? Can I get back to you? (Ambassadors are not expected to automatically become Table Captains).

If no: Thanks for considering it. I'm sorry you won't be able to be a Table Captain. Of course, we'd love to have you come as a guest to the event, even if you're not a Table Captain, and bring anyone else you'd like.

Note the middle section that contains the wording you want each Table Captain to use when inviting their guests.

- Second are those guests who were invited to your Points of Entry by a non-Ambassador, be it a volunteer, a board member, a staff member, or someone else in the community. Similarly, the person in your organization who has had the most contact with each of the other well-cultivated Point of Entry guests calls them personally to invite them to the Ask Event and carefully assigns them to the ideal Table Captain.

Preparing Your Table Captains

Whether or not your Table Captains have been successful Ambassadors in the prior year, this is the Table Captain Welcome Letter we recommend you send every new Table Captain as they sign on. Note the middle section that contains the wording you want each Table Captain to use when inviting their guests. Using this wording is critical to the success of your event. Guests need to be told in advance that while the event is free of charge, they will be asked to give money at the end of the hour, although there is no expected minimum gift. In other words, it is fine for people to give nothing at all.

TABLE CAPTAIN WELCOME LETTER
BENEVON FREE ONE-HOUR ASK EVENT

Thank you for agreeing to be a Table Captain at our upcoming event, (name of event), to be held on (date, location, time). (Can give more background here about the type of event, what the money will be used for, etc.)

The Table Captains are the most essential element in ensuring the success of the event. This packet is intended to provide you with everything you will need to make your job easier and more enjoyable. Please take the time to familiarize yourself with the contents.

As a Table Captain, you have agreed to fill a table of 10 people, including yourself. We recommend that you invite the people who have been to a Point of Entry as your guest and who expressed interest in becoming more involved.

In order to have a full table of 10 people on the day of the event, we ask that you pre-confirm 14 guests. The more personal the invitation, the better. We advise inviting people in person or by telephone, then confirming by mailing them one of the postcards provided in this packet. Please plan to call them once more about a week before the event to reconfirm yet again.

Keep a separate list of those who are unable to attend or call to cancel at the last minute. We would like to send them materials about our program.

Here is some suggested wording you might want to use in inviting your guests:

"Hello, ___________, I'd like to invite you to join me at my table at the ________ event. This is a free breakfast for people to come and learn more about our organization. Yes, it is a fundraiser, too. You will be asked to consider making a contribution. There is no minimum and no maximum gift requested. It will be the job of the organization to inspire people to want to give. As much as anything, we want people to come and find out about the great programs offered. I would be delighted if you could join me."

Please fax or mail your confirmed guest list (on the form provided) to the _________ office by (date).

We have also attached a list of all the scheduled introductory tours of the organization before the big event. We encourage you to invite your guests to visit the program firsthand.

Please feel free to contact ________________ at any time should you have further questions or need additional materials.

Again, thank you for serving as a Table Captain. Your participation enables us to continue the important work of ________________________________.

Finally, here is our Table Captain Job Description, which includes their duties on the day of the Ask Event. The key job of your Table Captains is to fill a table of 10 on the day of the event. This requires each Table Captain to start by inviting many more than 10 guests and by confirming at least 14 people personally (with reminder e-mails, postcards, and phone calls) at least two times as the event approaches, including once the day before the event. That is what it will take to produce 10 people at their table on the day of your event.

TABLE CAPTAIN JOB DESCRIPTION
BENEVON FREE ONE-HOUR ASK EVENT

1. Fill table of 10 guests at Ask Event. (This will mean confirming 14 guests by reminding them personally by phone or e-mail the day before.)
2. Make sure that at least 50% (ideally, 100%) of guests have attended a Point of Entry in the year prior to the Ask Event.
3. Mail save-the-date cards to each guest as they accept your invitation.
4. Keep a separate list of those unable to attend who have said they would like to receive more information about the organization.
5. Submit final guest list to the organization by three weeks before the Ask Event.
6. Arrive at the event at least 30 minutes early to greet your guests and pick up your Table Captain day-of-event packet.
7. Pass out pledge cards and envelopes as instructed during the pitch.
8. Set an example for your guests by enjoying the event and filling out your own pledge card at this time. Guests will be looking to you at that moment to see what they are supposed to do.
9. Collect completed pledge cards and envelopes from your guests and return them to the Table Captain check-in table before you leave the event.
10. Call your guests within two days to thank them for coming and get their impressions and feedback. (Do not ask them for money.)

The Ask Event Program

Now, we will walk through each element of the Ask Event program. As with everything else in the Benevon Model, do not be tempted to deviate from these specifications, even though some of them may seem counterintuitive. This event is choreographed like a theatrical production and every single one of your 60 minutes counts.

Program Elements

Here is a program outline for the Free One-Hour Ask Event.

PROGRAM
BENEVON FREE ONE-HOUR ASK EVENT

Background music as guests arrive

Welcome and Thank You – 3 minutes; board chair or emcee thanks board members, Table Captains, visiting dignitaries; shares personal connection; recognizes event sponsor

Opening Emotional Hook – 3 minutes; invocation, poem or audio PSA, song

Eat and Socialize – 10 minutes; emcee calls attention to centerpieces or vignettes / fact sheets in programs and to the souvenirs being passed around

Visionary Leader – 5 minutes; personal connection, results, vision for the future; creates the gap

Video – 7 minutes; emotion!

Testimonials – 1 or 2 different perspectives; 3 minutes each; facts and inspiration, credibility; may use interview format

Pitch – 5 minutes; Board Member or Volunteer: states personal connection to mission quickly; walks the audience through the pledge card (includes time for guests to fill out the card and pass in to the Table Captain); no background music or PowerPoint screens. Must agree to read the script as written and rehearse

Wrap Up – 1 minute; emcee thanks them again for their support and invites to Point of Entry

Background music plays as soon as event officially ends

You want your guests to know right away that you have something meaningful and important to tell them about; you did not just invite them to have breakfast.

As the guests arrive, they are greeted by volunteers, students, or program participants, who guide them to the nametag table. As they find their table in the ballroom, they join their friend the Table Captain and take their seats. Music is playing in the background. There is an air of excitement.

Welcome and Thank You (3 minutes)

The event begins at exactly the designated start time with a welcome and thank you from the board chair or a key volunteer, someone who has a direct connection to the organization.

Do not expect everyone to be in their seats waiting for the event to begin. There may still be many empty seats. Tempted as you may be to delay due to low attendance at the start time, do not start late. It will throw off the timing of the entire event. The first part of the script for the welcome includes thanking the board members, Table Captains, and any special guests. During these first few minutes of introductions, many more guests will arrive.

Opening Emotional Hook (3 minutes)

While the term "Emotional Hook" may sound crass, this element is essential to the program. It is designed to connect people emotionally to your mission within the first five minutes of the event. You want your guests to know right away that you have something meaningful and important to tell them about; you did not just invite them to have breakfast. This opening Emotional Hook could be a child reading a poem, a candle-lighting ceremony, someone singing a song related to the mission, or an inspiring invocation. One domestic violence group played a recording of a 911 emergency call, and another group showed the video of their new 30-second public service announcement. The opening Emotional Hook sets the tone for the entire event; it wakes people up to your mission and piques their interest for more.

Again, the purpose is not to give people a valuable object, but rather to connect them to real people who are involved with your organization even during this 10 minutes of down time.

Eating and Socializing (10 minutes)

This is the only "down time" in the one-hour program. People need a few minutes to socialize and connect with other guests at their table. The moderator has told them the program will start back up in 10 minutes and encouraged them to look at their table tents (folded-over pieces of paper) in front of each person's place, displaying something that personalizes the work of the organization and educates people about the mission. For example, one American Lung Association event had photos of kids at asthma camp with stories by each child of why they look forward all year long to going to asthma camp. Other groups have cards with statistics about homelessness and stories about homeless families, or percentages of various toxic chemicals contained in certain foods and stories of the human impact. People are encouraged to pass these cards around so others can learn from them as well.

This social time is also the part of the program where the guests receive small gifts, delivered personally to their tables by a volunteer, program participant, or family member. Again, the purpose is not to give people a valuable object, but rather to connect them to real people who are involved with your organization even during this 10 minutes of down time. Think about what you could give people that would tie into your program and your mission and how it could be delivered or presented to them as they sit at their tables.

For example, the same event that had the stories about asthma camp had camp-aged kids passing around plastic straws in beautiful little cellophane bags with bows. Later in the program, the testimonial speaker asked guests to open the bags, take out the straws and squeeze them until they were partially closed and then inhale through them, to experience what it feels like to have an asthma attack.

One group serving homebound, rural, elderly individuals passed out holiday greeting cards and pens and asked

One group serving homebound, rural, elderly individuals passed out holiday greeting cards and pens and asked the event guests to write a card to one of the people they serve.

the event guests to write a card to one of the people they serve. Other gifts may be less experiential, like apples, pens, bookmarks, pins, and buttons.

Visionary Leader Talk (5 minutes)

Now it is time for the leader of the organization to share the vision for the future. The Visionary Leader Talk is the anchor element of your Ask Event. It is worth taking the time to craft it carefully and to rehearse it several times, coaching your Visionary Leader to deliver the talk powerfully, following the script.

This talk lasts five minutes. Like the Visionary Leader Talk at the Point of Entry, this talk conveys the leader's personal story and connection to the mission, one key accomplishment in each of the three bucket areas, and the gap between where your organization is now and where you need to go in order to fulfill the next phase of your mission. This talk is delivered with emotion.

Video (7 minutes)

A video is essential at your Ask Event. We refer to this as a seven-minute, "three-cry" video. This is because the main job of the video is to inspire people about the human impact of your work and move them to tears. It brings to light, in an emotional way, the deeper work of the organization. People should be noticeably moved, not necessarily because they feel sad or upset, but because they have been touched. Perhaps the video made them laugh, or reminded them of all they have to be thankful for. First and foremost, the video must move people.

Most groups err on the side of too little emotion, feeling it is unprofessional or in some way insulting to the people they serve or the work they do. However, emotion is so key to fundraising that most people are not even conscious of

For the purpose of your Ask Event, do not be tempted to make a stand-alone, highly professional, narrated video, one that tells everything your organization does.

the degree to which their emotions drive their charitable giving. If you don't capture people's hearts as well as their minds, you will never have lifelong donors.

The video should include three first-person stories, one representing each of your buckets or areas of impact. Close-up shots of people telling their own stories are best. There is no need for any narration. Background music can be highly effective.

For the purpose of your Ask Event, do not be tempted to make a stand-alone, highly professional, narrated video, one that tells everything your organization does. Remember that this seven-minute video will be part of a 60-minute program, with many other program elements to educate and inspire people about your work. The sole purpose of this video is to give people a powerful, succinct, emotionally riveting experience of your mission in action. As people watch this video on a large screen in a big room with the lights turned down, they will feel the impact right in their chairs.

Testimonials (6 minutes)

There is no substitute for a live testimonial. A firsthand account of how your organization changed a life is the most powerful statement of the impact of your work. It must leave people so deeply moved and reminded of what is truly important in life that they feel compelled to take action.

We allow a maximum of six minutes for the testimonial(s) at the Ask Event. There are several options for how to use this time. Most groups have one or, at most, two testimonial speakers. If your speaker is nervous, shy, or too young to be trusted with a microphone, the testimonial may be delivered in an interview format. One person close to the organization is designated as the interviewer. The testimonial speaker knows in advance the questions they will be asked and has rehearsed this conversation with the interviewer.

The Pitch Person should not be trying to convince anyone to give.

The ideal testimonial speaker is someone who has had a firsthand experience of your organization's work—a client or family member, a longtime arts lover, or one or two alumni of your school or program.

The testimonial talk follows the three-part Essential Story format (see page 130): what life was like before this person became involved with the organization, what services or intervention the organization offered that changed things for the person, and what life is like now, including how this person is able to give back to others.

You will need to script and rehearse your testimonial speakers to be sure they speak passionately and stay within their allocated time.

Pitch (5 minutes)

The Ask Event culminates in the pitch. It is now 50 minutes into the 60-minute program. People were told when they were invited to the event that they would be asked for money. At this point, 40% to 50% of the people are ready to give. They want to know how to go about making a financial contribution right now. The remaining 50% to 60% of the people are not ready to give at the event. They may end up giving the next day, the next week, the next year, or not at all. They may want to go home and talk it over with others, come to a Point of Entry themselves or with others, transfer money or property first, or meet with the board or committee. Or they may decide not to get involved with your organization at all. They may have other issues they are more involved with at this time.

The job of the Pitch Person at the Ask Event is to focus on the people who are ready to give and to tell them how to go about that. The Pitch Person should not be trying to convince anyone to give. We refer to the Pitch Person as a "credible, school teacher-like" person: "credible" because they are truly tied to the organization's mission, and "school teacher-like" because they will follow a script. They understand that their job is to walk people through the pledge card and help them to give.

Do not assume that you need a big-name person in your community to be your Pitch Person. In fact, the ideal Pitch Person may be more of a "regular" person than a superstar. A parent or other family member who is a good public speaker can be an excellent Pitch Person. A long-standing, dedicated board member or member of your Sustainable Funding Team is often ideal. So long as they are truly passionate about your mission, will not deviate from the script, and are comfortable speaking in front of an audience, you will have made a good choice. Although it probably does not need to be said, I will say it anyway: the Pitch Person may not be someone on the paid staff of the organization.

Here is the Pitch Script to be followed:

BENEVON PITCH SCRIPT YEAR ONE FREE ONE-HOUR ASK EVENT

Thanks to both of you for those great stories!

Hi, I'm (your name). (Answer two questions: Why are you involved with the organization? What is your role in the organization? Answer both questions with no more than two sentences.)

Today you've heard the full (name of organization) story and met some of our wonderful people, and it's my privilege to ask you to make a financial investment to support our day-to-day operations. This is not just an investment in (name of organization); it truly is an investment in our own futures, and I believe that it is one of the most important investments that any of us can make.

To build a stronger foundation for expanding our programs and to provide a stable future for (name of organization), today we are launching a brand new partnership—the ______________ ("Dream Builder Society"). If you have been inspired by what you've seen today, I ask you to consider joining me this morning as a founding member of our Society.

BENEVON PITCH SCRIPT YEAR ONE
FREE ONE-HOUR ASK EVENT

Optional Insert for Leadership Gift:
We have something very exciting to announce. (Name of donor/s) has made a generous Leadership Gift of $__________ to support our work.

Optional Insert for Challenge Gift:
We have something very exciting to announce. (Name of donor/s or "a generous donor or group of donors") has made a generous gift to challenge us all today to support (name of organization). (Then explain clearly what will be matched and up to what $ limit.)

Now I'd like to ask the Table Captains to pass out the pledge cards. *Pause only briefly*

Starting at the top of the card, the Dream Builder pledge level names are meant to give you a sense of what your contribution can do. Your contribution will go toward the unrestricted operating funds of (name of organization).

1. The first giving level, Building Hope, is a pledge of $1,000 each year for five years, which is approximately $83 per month. Your gift would let us provide mentoring help to one new child, like (someone you met in the program) for each of the next five years.
2. The next giving level, our Creating Dreams level, is a pledge of $10,000 a year for five years. You would allow us to match even more kids like..., plus support the friendships that graduates from our program continue into future years.
3. The last level, Changing Lives, is a pledge of $25,000 a year for five years. We would be able to provide weekly relationship-building support, recreational activities, life-skills workshops, academic support, and career-building activities to youth in need throughout our area.

If you are joining me today as a founding member of the Dream Builder Society, my personal thanks for your generous support!

Although I started by introducing the Dream Builder Society, we know and respect that you may prefer to give at a different level, and so we provide the next line just for you. On this line, please tell us how much you would like to give and for how many years.

We truly appreciate whatever level of support you can provide and we ask that you make the first payment on your pledge today.

Perhaps you would like to consider a gift of stock or something else. Or you simply have some great ideas for us. If so, please check the next box, the one that says, "Please contact me. I have other thoughts to share."

As you are filling out your card, please know that whatever you gave, including the gift of your time, we sincerely appreciate your support for the kids we serve.

When you are finished, please pass your envelopes back to your Table Captain.

Now, I'll turn the program back to _______ to wrap up.

The Pitch Person tells the Table Captains when to pass out the pledge cards, envelopes, and pens to each guest. After walking the audience through each line on the pledge sheet, instructing them how to fill out the form, and giving them time to do that, the Pitch Person directs the guests to pass their envelopes back to the Table Captain.

PLEDGE CARD

BENEVON FREE ONE-HOUR ASK EVENT

Organization Name
Name of Event
Fundraising (Breakfast/Lunch)

I would like to become a founding member of the (Multiple-Year Giving Society):

___ (First Unit of Service): $1,000 per year for 5 years
___ (Second Unit of Service): $10,000 per year for 5 years
___ (Third Unit of Service): $25,000 per year for 5 years

I would like to contribute in other ways:

___ Contribute $______ for ___ years.
___ Please contact me. I have other thoughts to share.

Payment:

___ My check is enclosed, made payable to: ______________________
___ Please charge my Visa/MC # ______________________ Exp. ________
___ Please contact me about paying my pledge with stock.
___ My company will match my gift.

We will bill you in (month) for your annual pledge, unless you request otherwise.

Signature: ______________________

Date: ______________________

Name: ______________________

Organization ______________________

Address: ______________________

City: ______________ State: __________ Zip: __________

Day Phone: ______________ Evening Phone: ______________

Email: ______________________

Even if the Table Captains have already made a financial contribution to the organization, they need to be writing something on their pledge cards during the pitch.

The Table Captains have another essential role during the pitch. They must set the example for their guests by filling out their pledge cards at this time. Even if the Table Captains have already made a financial contribution to the organization, they need to be writing something on their pledge cards during the pitch. The guests will glance at the Table Captains and follow their lead.

Wrap Up (1 minute)

The emcee or board chair thanks everyone for coming and for their support for the organization. People are invited to linger and chat if they like. The background music comes on and the event ends, right on time, in 60 minutes.

Rehearsing

To improve the likelihood that your program will flow smoothly and that each element will be strong and effective unto itself, it is essential to have a full rehearsal of the event program one to three days prior to the event, in the actual location where the event will take place.

Ask Event Follow-Up

The two-week period after the Ask Event is, by far, the most fertile time for additional fundraising as well as cultivation of your new Multiple-Year Donors. This is not the time for the event organizers to go on vacation! While you may be tired and ready for a break, your guests on the other hand have just gotten interested. Now is the time they are curious and eager to learn more. This post-event follow-up can be the most exciting and productive part of the process. If you have followed the Benevon Model closely, and especially if there was enough emotion present in your Ask Event program, there will be much more ripened fruit to be picked in these critical weeks.

Many organizations create a Post-Ask Event Follow-Up Call form or template that team members can complete after each contact with a donor or potential interested party.

The Follow-Up Calls after the Ask Event follow the same outline as the Post-Point of Entry calls.

Who Makes the Follow-Up Calls

The calls should be made by a high-level core group of two or three "insiders" who attended the Ask Event. These are the people who are senior enough in the organization so as to make the guests feel special. Their main role will be to thank people and to listen well for the cues about how that person wants to be cultivated.

Managing the Follow-Up Call Data

Establish a system for the Ask Event follow-up to make sure that all information, including referrals and "thoughts to share," ends up in your central database. Many organizations create a Post-Ask Event Follow-Up Call form or template that team members can complete after each contact with a donor or potential interested party.

Who Must Be Called

You will not need to call every Ask Event guest. Only call the following groups of attendees in this order of priority.

All Table Captains

Call all Table Captains within 24 hours of the Ask Event. For a breakfast event, call on the same day. Use the Five-Step Follow-Up Call process, modified as follows:

- Thank the Table Captain. It was their hard work that filled the event and ultimately made it so successful.

- Ask your Table Captains: "What did you think of the event? What did you hear from your guests?" You are listening for comments about guests who took their

A voicemail message from the Table Captains to their guests is fine, just be sure the Table Captains know not to ask their guests for money in this call.

pledge card with them and told their Table Captain, "I have to discuss this with someone else, but I really want to support this organization." When you hear these comments, add these people to your personal phone call follow-up list.

- Encourage your Table Captains to call all of their guests to thank them for attending. A voicemail message from the Table Captains to their guests is fine, just be sure the Table Captains know not to ask their guests for money in this call. If the guest was excited about the mission of the organization, the Table Captain should invite them to attend an upcoming Point of Entry Event if they have not yet done so. This may be your public Point of Entry Event or a private one that the Table Captain hosts.

- If the Table Captains are very excited about how the Ask Event went, ask, "Is there any other way you would like to become more involved with us? Is there any other way you would like to participate?" Listen closely to their responses. Then, ask: "Is there anyone else you can think of that we ought to invite to a __________ (Point of Entry Event)?" Suggest that they invite those people to a Point of Entry Event between now and next year, and if they themselves have not attended one, invite them to do so. Tell them that their feedback about the Point of Entry would be very helpful, and tell them when the next one is scheduled to take place. If appropriate, ask, "Would you like to be an Ambassador going forward? An Ambassador is someone who invites friends to Point of Entry Events."

If the donors are very excited about the work of the organization, ask if they would like to become more involved.

All Multiple-Year Donors

Call all your new Multiple-Year Donors the day of the Ask Event or the next day. Customize the Five-Step Follow-Up Call process as follows:

- Thank them sincerely for their contribution. Make them feel special for joining the Multiple-Year Giving Society and taking a leadership role. Tell them what their gift will make possible for your organization, using real examples.

- Ask, "What did you think of the event?" Listen closely to their responses. If they have any specific concerns (about the food, the venue, the program, for example), acknowledge those concerns and thank them for their honest feedback.

- If the donors are very excited about the work of the organization, ask if they would like to become more involved. Is there any other way they would like to participate? Listen closely to their responses. Also ask if they would like to be an Ambassador—someone who opens doors in the community and brings people to Points of Entry.

- Ask, "Is there anyone else you can think of that we ought to invite to a _________ (Point of Entry Event)?" Suggest that they invite those people to one sometime between now and next year's Ask Event. If they have not attended a Point of Entry Event themselves, invite them to do so. If they have not attended a Point of Entry Event themselves, invite them to do so.

Next, contact the people who indicated, "I have other thoughts to share" on their pledge card.

- If you have an upcoming Free Feel-Good Cultivation Event scheduled for large donors, tell them a little bit about it to pique their interest and ask them to save the date.

- Let them know that they will be invited to one or two mission-related events for donors per year because they are now part of your____________ (Multiple-Year Giving Society).

- Ask, "Can we give you a call from time to time to get your thoughts or advice on related issues? Sometimes we are too close to things and need a fresh perspective from someone who appreciates our mission."

"Thoughts to Share" People

Next, contact the people who indicated, "I have other thoughts to share" on their pledge card. Thank them for coming, and ask, "What are your thoughts? What ideas do you have?" During this time, listen and take notes. Then thank them for their ideas and suggestions, and let them know what your next steps will be.

If they are very excited about the work of the organization, ask if they would like to become more involved. Is there any other way they would like to participate? Listen closely to their responses.

Ask, "Is there anyone else you can think of that we ought to invite to a _________ (Point of Entry Event)?" Suggest that they invite those people to one between now and next year. If they have not attended a Point of Entry Event themselves, invite them to do so. Tell them that their feedback about the Point of Entry would be very helpful, and tell them when the next one is scheduled to take place.

For those no-shows who had been well cultivated, you can ask them in that phone call to join your Multiple-Year Giving Society at one of your larger levels.

All Other Donors

Contact all other donors including smaller-pledge donors and one-year-only donors. Decide on a "cut-off" dollar amount, and call the higher-level donors. Use these same modified Follow-Up Call steps. Thank them sincerely for their gifts.

No-Shows

Contact all those people who were expected at the Ask Event but did not come. You will know who these people are because their nametags will have been left on the nametag table at the Ask Event. Divide your list into two groups.

First, contact donors and friends of the organization who have already been well cultivated and are ready to be asked, but were unable to attend the Ask Event. Call each of these people and say, "We missed you at the event; here are some of the highlights from the event." You can then include quotes from the Visionary Leader speech or offer to send a copy of the video to the people on this list. "We launched the Multiple-Year Giving Society to ensure the financial strength of our organization and the sustainability of our work in the community." For those no-shows who had been well cultivated, you can ask them in that phone call to join your Multiple-Year Giving Society at one of your larger levels.

Second, contact those no-shows you do not know at all, those for whom the Ask Event would have been a Point of Entry Event. These names should be collected and reviewed at a subsequent board, staff, or volunteer meeting to determine who has connections with these people and could call and invite them to a Point of Entry Event.

You may follow up by mail with those people who attended the Ask Event but did not give, however you do not have permission to call them.

Those Who Did Not Give

You may follow up by mail with those people who attended the Ask Event but did not give, however you do not have permission to call them. These people are still on your Cultivation Superhighway. Just because they did not give at the event does not mean that they aren't interested in your organization. Remember, the Ask Event was a Pre-Point of Entry for many people. Now you need to take steps to find out how to cultivate these people—with their permission—so that they might become volunteers or donors later.

Send a letter to thank these guests for attending the event. Tell them you really appreciate their support, and hope they found the event informative and inspiring. Invite them to attend a Point of Entry Event and include dates of upcoming Point of Entry Events and instructions on how to RSVP. If you do not hear back from them, "bless-and-release" them. Do not add them to your direct mail list.

Follow-Up is Critical

After all the work you have done to put on a successful Ask Event, do not skip over this critical Post-Ask Event Follow-Up process.

This completes the 12 steps for implementing the Benevon Model. Let's look next at how to integrate your other fundraising events into the model—by "missionizing" them.

CHAPTER 16

WHAT COMES NEXT: CUSTOMIZING A SYSTEM OF EVENTS FOR YOUR ORGANIZATION

Now that you have an overview of the Benevon Model for Sustainable Funding, I trust you can see the potential of this mission-centered approach for your organization. You may already be thinking about how you could convert many of your more labor-intensive, stand-alone special events into events that can advance not only your mission, but also your system for building sustainable funding from lifelong donors. You may also be more open to the idea of phasing out or eliminating existing events.

Before we can talk about how to "missionize" each of your existing events (that is, make them more mission-centered), we need to step back and review our Benevon classification of events.

In our model, any event your organization is now putting on can be recast to fit into one of the following categories:

1. The classic Point of Entry Event and its three variations:
   - The Point of Entry in a Box
   - The Pre-Point of Entry
   - The One-on-One Point of Entry

Each event is followed by a personal Follow-Up Call to ask for the guest's feedback about the event and determine their level of interest in moving forward with you.

2. The Free One-Hour Ask Event
3. The Free Feel-Good Cultivation Event
4. The Point of Entry Conversion Event

As we go through these descriptions, notice the elements that are common to each event. There is one similar theme to them all: your organization's mission! Each event includes facts, emotion, and the capturing of names of the interested guests, with their permission. Each event is followed by a personal Follow-Up Call to ask for the guest's feedback about the event and determine their level of interest in moving forward with you.

The Classic Point of Entry Event

The cornerstone of the Benevon Model, this free, one-hour, get-acquainted event educates and inspires people about your mission. People are invited word-of-mouth by a friend or colleague who is an Ambassador for your organization to a small gathering of 10 to 15 people, where they are educated and inspired about your work. They are told in advance that they will be receiving one phone call after the event to ask for their feedback, not their money. These events are held at least twice a month, rain or shine, all year long.

The carefully crafted, high-touch, low-tech program, which includes a greeting from a board member, a Visionary Leader Talk, and a tour of your mission filled with myth-buster facts and succinct, powerful stories and testimonials, moves guests to tears and leaves them wanting to get on the phone to tell people what they just saw and learned. It should be a life-changing event for each guest, whether or not they choose to become more involved with your group.

In the follow-up process after each Point of Entry Event, you should aim to very naturally recruit at least one new Ambassador.

At that point, your organization can begin to offer "portable" events we refer to as Points of Entry in a Box, which can be hosted by Ambassadors in conference rooms, living rooms, church halls, etc.

Point of Entry Events: Three Variations

There are three variations to the classic Point of Entry Event, which you will be able to offer as you become more comfortable with the Benevon Model.

The Point of Entry in a Box

After you have put on at least 10 of your classic Point of Entry Events in your main office or center, you will have tested and refined the format. By then, it should become so repeatable that you could almost put all of the key elements—the photos, props, and stories (everything except for the people, of course)—in a box and take it on the road.

At that point, your organization can begin to offer "portable" events we refer to as Points of Entry in a Box, which can be hosted by Ambassadors in conference rooms, living rooms, church halls, etc. Although you will still need to take the other speakers with you, the Point of Entry in a Box opens up many other venues and times of day to reach more people with your message.

Points of Entry in a Box work well for Ambassadors who have a natural venue and prefer to have you bring the Point of Entry Event to their location. Once your Ambassador program gets up and running smoothly, you should aim to have one of your two Points of Entry each month be a Point of Entry in a Box. And, just like after a classic Point of Entry Event in your organization's main office, you should expect to recruit at least one new Ambassador from each Point of Entry in a Box.

The Pre-Point of Entry

A first cousin to the classic Point of Entry Event is the Pre-Point of Entry. This category is not actually part of the Benevon Model, but I have made a placeholder for it here because so many people ask us what to call those events like civic club presentations, Rotary meetings, public infor-

Having that date set in advance and announced by a peer within the group can go a long way to turning a public talk into a Pre-Point of Entry Event.

mation sessions, nonprofit fairs at shopping malls, etc. At these events, the "guests" are not necessarily expecting any particular presentation from your group, nor would it be appropriate to contact each person afterwards, since they have not given express permission for you to do so.

People who give you a card at the end of your presentation at the Rotary meeting or people who express interest at a booth-style type of fair cannot be considered to have attended a true Point of Entry Event. However, if they give you their card or request a personal follow-up, you then have their permission to do a formal Follow-Up Call and invite them to come to your regularly scheduled Point of Entry Event.

While these public events can be very time consuming and may seem unproductive in terms of generating more Point of Entry guests and advancing your success in building sustainable funding, they can be worthwhile public relations activities, and we certainly encourage our groups to participate in them if they can find the time to prepare and attend.

One suggestion for making a service club meeting where you are speaking, like a Rotary meeting, more productive, while sticking to the Benevon Model, is to ask one Rotarian in advance (perhaps the one who invited you to speak there) if they would host a Point of Entry Event in the weeks following the Rotary meeting. Choose a date in advance and let that person stand up and announce it before and after your talk. Those interested in attending the full Point of Entry Event can let you or their fellow Rotarian know that at the end of the presentation. Having that date set in advance and announced by a peer within the group can go a long way to turning a public talk into a Pre-Point of Entry Event.

There is nothing phony or inauthentic about the process. There is no sales pitch. It rings true all the way through.

The One-on-One Point of Entry Event

As you present each element of your classic Point of Entry Event, it will start to shape the way you talk about your organization's work everywhere. Your board members and volunteers will begin to acquire a natural "elevator speech" from your Mission Message and people will realize that many of the elements of the Point of Entry Event could be consolidated into a One-on-One Point of Entry. Although this is not a substitute for a real Point of Entry, the myths, facts, storytelling, and needs can all be conveyed in a dialog between two people over the holiday punchbowl, sitting on an airplane, or standing in line at the grocery store. Suddenly each of your volunteers becomes a powerful ambassador for your work, spreading the word out in the community and generating more guests for your Points of Entry.

Passion is the Key

Whichever version of a Point of Entry Event a guest first attends, they will get a firsthand experience of your mission and your passion for the work of the organization. The people inviting their friends are passionate about your work. The people speaking at the Point of Entry Events are passionate. The stories about the people whose lives are changed by your work evoke more passion, inspiring the guests to introduce others. There is nothing phony or inauthentic about the process. There is no sales pitch. It rings true all the way through.

The Benevon Free One-Hour Ask Event

The second type of event in the Benevon Model is the Benevon Free One-Hour Ask Event. While other special events may resemble this, it is unlikely that they are identical to this event. Many aspects of the event are counterintuitive. This event can be done properly only in conjunction with the rest of the Benevon Model. In other words, it is not a stand-alone event.

To qualify as a Free One-Hour Ask Event in this model, at least 40% of the guests must have attended a Point of Entry Event in the prior year. Each guest is personally invited to the free breakfast or lunch Ask Event by a friend who has served as an Ambassador or by someone associated with the organization. The Table Captain tells them that they will be asked to give money at the event, but there is "no minimum and no maximum gift" expected. As much as anything, they are being asked to come and learn more about the organization.

The Ask Event provides a straightforward, time-limited immersion into the outstanding work of your organization. In one tightly choreographed hour, this event provides the same critical elements as the other events: the Facts 101, the Emotional Hook, and capturing names with permission. Beyond that, because a high percentage of the guests have attended your Points of Entry, the Ask Event includes a compelling Ask for multiple-year support at specific giving levels.

And again, just like after the other permission-based events, Benevon Follow-Up Calls are made right after the Ask Event, but not to everyone who attends—only to donors, Table Captains, and the guests who checked the last box on the pledge card, which says "Please contact me; I have other thoughts to share." These follow-up calls are an excellent opportunity to find new Ambassadors.

The Free Feel-Good Cultivation Event (Also Known as the Point of Re-Entry Event)

The third type of event in the Benevon Model is the Free Feel-Good Cultivation Event. The name pretty much says it all. These are the recognition and cultivation events for your Multiple-Year Giving Society Donors. Each event

The best Free Feel-Good Cultivation Events are mission-related program events that happen in the natural course of your organization's life.

must reconnect them to the Emotional Hook and reinforce the wisdom of their investment in your organization. That means these events always include a program or theme that ties to your mission.

Free Feel-Good Cultivation Events can take many forms:

- The best Free Feel-Good Cultivation Events are mission-related program events that happen in the natural course of your organization's life. Examples are graduations, science fair nights, special theater performances, and any other events you may already be having which honor your clients or families.
- In a second category are the specially planned, mission-related, invitation-only events, such as a special night for donors to serve dinner in your soup kitchen or the back-to-camp-for-grownups night.
- Third are the traditional recognition events, such as awards dinners or dinner parties in private homes, as long as they include a program with facts and emotion.
- In the fourth category are the formal or informal briefings or updates with a celebrity scientist or artist on their newest work or discovery.

These events can also be varied for donors at different giving levels. You may invite your biggest donors to an elegant dinner at the most exclusive private home with your CEO or a revered person in your field, if that is something they would enjoy. Your other Multiple-Year Giving Society Donors might be invited to a dinner or lecture series, a family picnic, or a special "environmental day."

Free Feel-Good Cultivation Events may also be used to introduce insiders to the next dream for the organization, such as a campaign for capital, major gifts, endowment, or a special program or project.

As for the best times of year to hold these events, the first one should be your Celebration Event, held four to six weeks after your Ask Event.

This event clearly includes the critical elements of the Facts 101 and the Emotional Hook, and capturing the names is usually not necessary because you already have the names of all the donors in attendance. After all, you invited them to the event!

Finally, just as with a Point of Entry Event and each of the other events, a Free Feel-Good Cultivation Event always engenders a Follow-Up Call, eliciting more feedback, which in turn enables you to further customize your approach to each donor. Use these calls to recruit new Ambassadors from your newly re-inspired Multiple-Year Donors. Every contact keeps the donor going around the cycle with you.

Planning Your Free Feel-Good Cultivation Events Strategically

I recommend a minimum of two Free Feel-Good Cultivation Events per year—one targeted to your highest Multiple-Year Giving Society Donors and one for all of your Multiple-Year Giving Society Donors. Ideally, you should also have a third event for all of your donors including those not in your Multiple-Year Giving Society.

As for the best times of year to hold these events, the first one should be your Celebration Event, held four to six weeks after your Ask Event. Invite everyone who has made your Ask Event a success: Ambassadors, Table Captains, your new Multiple-Year Giving Society Donors, board, and team members.

All other Free Feel-Good Cultivation Events should coincide with natural program events such as arts performances, graduations, and holiday celebrations.

Many groups are surprised to find they do not have existing Free Feel-Good Cultivation Events and they need to add one or two. They choose an existing program event and add a reception at the start. Free Feel-Good Cultivation Events are not designed to attract new friends to the organization,

The fourth type of event is what we call a Point of Entry Conversion Event. These are the traditional fundraising events, like the gala, the golf tournament, and the auction, which are retrofitted with a brief mission element.

but rather to cultivate your inner circle of Multiple-Year Giving Society Donors. Of course, these insiders are always encouraged to bring friends to the Free Feel-Good Cultivation Events as well, as long as the focus of the event really is on your loyal prior donors. For the new people, the event will serve as a Pre-Point of Entry Event. Just be sure to follow up with them to invite them—or better yet, have their friend invite them—to a Point of Entry Event.

Finally, do not underestimate the magic of a free event. If you inspire them at your Free Feel-Good Cultivation Event, people will remember you gave them something for free when it comes time to ask them for the next contribution. Just make sure you have one or more event sponsors who receive plenty of credit, so your loyal donors will know you did not spend any of their money to pay for this event.

Point of Entry Conversion Events

The fourth type of event is what we call a Point of Entry Conversion Event. These are the traditional fundraising events, like the gala, the golf tournament, and the auction, which are retrofitted with a brief mission element. *These events are not required at all in the Benevon Model. In fact, your goal should be to phase out as many of these events as possible, rather than converting them.*

Technically, these events should be considered Pre-Point of Entry Events, like the Rotary or civic club presentations mentioned earlier, since their only purpose in our model would be to interest the guests in attending your classic Point of Entry Events.

However, we give them a category of their own here, called Point of Entry Conversion Events, in order to mark them as distinct for the many groups who, when they first begin implementing the Benevon Model, are so are heavily

Question 1: What was the name of the organization for which the event was raising funds?

dependent on these entertainment-style fundraising events that they are reluctant to eliminate them immediately. As an interim solution, by inserting a well-crafted, brief, mission-focused element into the program and capturing the names of the people interested in learning more, that traditional, entertainment-style event can lead to follow-up and cultivation of a small segment of guests, who can then be invited to a "real" Point of Entry Event.

Having said that, converting a traditional fundraising event into a Point of Entry Conversion Event is still not nearly as efficient as inviting people to your real Point of Entry Events where they will know what they have been invited to: the entire program will be about your mission, and you will have permission to follow up with everyone.

How Effective are Your Existing Fundraising Events?

Assuming there are some events you feel you must keep, at least for the next year, here is a simple test to see if you have successfully inserted the mission and converted each traditional fundraising event into a Point of Entry Conversion Event: the day after the event, if someone were to ask your guests about the dinner-dance or the golf tournament, could the guests have answered the following two-question pop quiz?

Question 1: What was the name of the organization for which the event was raising funds?

While they may well remember how much they enjoyed the golf or the dinner-dance or the nice conversation they had with a friend, will they be able to recall the name of the organization that worked so hard to produce the event and ultimately received their financial support?

If you want to quickly convey your mission, have a short testimonial from someone who has benefited from your work. That is what people will remember most.

Question 2: What does that organization do?

Even if your name is well known in your community, do not assume that people truly know about the breadth of your programs. If you want to quickly convey your mission, have a short testimonial from someone who has benefited from your work. That is what people will remember most.

The easiest way to do this is to insert a Point of Entry element into the sit-down portion of your fundraising event. At the banquet after your golf tournament, the board chair might stand up and thank everyone for coming, acknowledge the great day of golf, and then say something like this: "We here at the Mentor Project would not be doing our jobs if we didn't take advantage of the fact that we have you all gathered here today to tell you a little bit about our program." Then have your executive director get up and give the Visionary Leader Talk like the one given at the Point of Entry Events, followed by a brief, live testimonial from a person whose life has been changed thanks to the work of your organization. With good preparation, this can all be accomplished in 10 minutes. Wrap that up with the board member thanking the audience and saying, "We know many of you did not know much about the Mentor Project before you came here today. If you would like to find out more, your table host would love to invite you to one of the special tours we've organized just for today's golfers. There's a card under your plate. Please check out those dates and let your host know tonight which date you'd like to attend."

The same strategy can be used at a gala, where the table hosts each schedule a Point of Entry Event to take place a week or two after the fundraising event. Have your emcee reference these future Points of Entry right after the testimonial speaker's talk during the mission-related element of the event and encourage each guest to talk to their table host

What is the simplest, most streamlined and effective package of events that you could leave as a legacy for your organization?

for details. That way, interested guests will have a specific event hosted by a friend they can plan to attend.

Again, you can see that the Point of Entry Conversion Event must include the same critical elements as the Point of Entry; namely, it must include the Facts 101, the Emotional Hook, and a mechanism for capturing the names of the guests with their permission. Finally, you must plan in advance when you will be making the Follow-Up Calls after these events. Start by calling all the table hosts to see what feedback they received from their guests, including names of any guests who expressed interest in attending a Point of Entry Event. While these events will likely not be as productive as a true Point of Entry Event, the strategies I am suggesting are designed to help you tell your story and capture even a few names of people who want to know more.

Over time, as you have more success with the Benevon Model for Sustainable Funding, you may gradually phase out these events, using the valuable staff time for major donor cultivation activities instead of party planning.

The Ideal System

Now that you understand the event classification within the Benevon Model and how the events you are currently producing could be "missionized," let's look at how to design the ideal System of Events for your organization.

As you go through this process, think ahead all the way to your goal. What is the simplest, most streamlined and effective package of events that you could leave as a legacy for your organization? What are the most mission-focused events that you would want to have take place year after year, each time infused with new stories that educate and inspire?

Note: there are no Point of Entry Conversion Events or Pre-Point of Entry Events in this ideal schema.

For right now, do not be concerned about how you will get from here to there. Merely tell the truth about what "there" should look like. Think from the perspective of your organization's mission. Which package of events would most honor that mission, rather than hide it or cheapen it?

The ideal System of Events for organizations using the Benevon Model consists of:

- A minimum of two Point of Entry Events per month. Most groups settle on one classic Point of Entry at their office or program site per month, plus one or two Points of Entry in a Box per month.
- Only one Free One-Hour Ask Event per year.
- Two to three Free Feel-Good Cultivation Events per year. One is for your highest level Multiple-Year Giving Society Donors and the other is for all your Multiple-Year Giving Society Donors. A third Free Feel-Good Cultivation Event is also recommended for all donors (not just those in your Multiple-Year Giving Society).

Note: there are no Point of Entry Conversion Events or Pre-Point of Entry Events in this ideal schema.

Creating Your System of Events

To begin designing your System of Events, list all of your current events in the first column of the chart below. This list should include existing fundraising events as well as program events, classes for your participants and staff, volunteer recruitment events, events to recruit blood donors, staff recognition parties, etc. Do not limit yourself to the obvious fundraising events only.

CREATING YOUR SYSTEM OF EVENTS

Current Events	Convert Event to:			Ideal Month	Add/ Convert/ Eliminate by When
	Point of Entry Event Tour Stop	Point of Entry Conversion Event	Free Feel-Good Cultivation Event		
1.					
2.					
3.					
4.					
5.					
6.					
7.					
8.					
9.					
10.					

Next, while you are alone reading this, without your staff, board, or event committee at your side, take the time to answer this Soul-Searching Questions worksheet honestly for each of the events your organization currently produces.

What if someone just walked in and wrote you a check for your total goal? Would you still have the event?

Soul-Searching Questions

1. Why are you having the event, anyway?
2. Is there really an expectation that this event will raise money?
3. What have you said in the past to justify not reaching your dollar goal for this event?
4. How attached are you and your organization to this type of event?
5. What if someone just walked in and wrote you a check for your total goal? Would you still have the event?
6. Thinking ahead to your next big event, if you don't make your goal, what will be the reason?
7. If the event is supposed to be a fundraiser, do you know how much it actually nets?
8. How many volunteers did it really take to put the event on?
9. If you have a dedicated fundraising staff, what else could they have been doing with the same amount of time and energy to bring in more money than the event nets?
10. For how many months in advance have you and your team been obsessing about the event?
11. What fixed costs, if any, must you meet?
12. Is this the right kind of event for your organization?
13. Does this type of event have sufficient metrics to predict and manage its financial results?
14. Is this event the best way to maximize the giving potential of each donor?
15. What would you think if you had to sit through the program for this event?
16. What are you building for future years by having this event?
17. On a scale of 1 to 10, how excited are you about producing this event?

Tell the truth about the real purpose and value of each of your existing events as you review your list. You are crafting your ideal lasting plan.

Finally, having answered these soul-searching questions for each event, look to each column on the chart, starting with the second column: Point of Entry Event Tour Stop. Decide which of your existing programs or activities might work for a Point of Entry Event as a tour stop representing one of your "buckets," as described in Chapter 10. For a school, that might be a holiday music concert. For a food bank, it might be Friday volunteer day, where senior volunteers pack food into backpacks to be delivered to schools for children to take home for the weekends.

Looking at the next column on the chart, which of your existing fundraising events can be slated for "missionization" and turned into a Point of Entry Conversion Event?

Tell the truth about the real purpose and value of each of your existing events as you review your list. You are crafting your ideal lasting plan.

Moving to the Free Feel-Good Cultivation Events column, what contenders do you have for that category? These would be events with a heartfelt, mission-based program already built into them, such as a graduation ceremony from your English as a Second Language program, or a homecoming reception or reunion to honor your overseas mission volunteers. Perhaps these are existing mission-related "fundraising" events, in the sense that you sell tickets to attend them—say, an annual volunteer recognition awards dinner. How can you get the cost of these events underwritten so they can now become free for attendees? You don't need to have more than two of these events, so don't overburden yourself here.

Blessing-and-Releasing Events

Let's look next at the events on your list that have not been selected for conversion thus far. These are the events that most likely need to be "blessed-and-released"—like your

In the long run, eliminating several events will allow you to grow a significant major gifts program, which is the missing steppingstone for most nonprofits that are serious about building sustainable funding.

Point of Entry guests who you respectfully let go—either gradually or immediately. These tend to be the fundraising events that are not even worth converting to Point of Entry Conversion Events because they do not reap enough in dollars or goodwill to justify the time and effort needed to produce them.

It is fine to have a sentimental moment of silence for each event as you bless-and-release it. While it may have served you well up to now, the time spent on putting on that beautiful event, moving forward, can be used for follow-up and cultivation of people who have been educated and inspired about your work and have given you their express permission to keep contacting them after a Point of Entry, Ask Event, or Free Feel-Good Cultivation Event. This is precious time you will need to cultivate these individuals personally. Many of them will become major donors.

In the long run, eliminating several events will allow you to grow a significant major gifts program, which is the missing steppingstone for most nonprofits that are serious about building sustainable funding.

You may be surprised to see what a difference it will make just to check the box that says you are *planning* to eliminate an event. Just like when you bless-and-release a Point of Entry guest or a potential donor, paradoxically, new possibilities seem to open up. You may suddenly see many other ways to retain the best elements of the event (often by blending them into another event) without needing to keep the original event intact.

One popular solution is to find a great community group that will take over hosting and producing the event and just invite you to speak as part of the event program, where they will present you with the check for the net proceeds of the event. We call that a "third party" event.

Before you fill in the last column, stating by when you will eliminate these events, let's talk about setting up your annual rotation of events. Then you will be ready to design your System of Events.

Aligning Your Events Correctly Throughout the Year

As you map out the years ahead using the Benevon Model, you must first decide when to hold your annual Ask Event. Everything else will revolve around that. The most popular times of the year for an Ask Event are the spring (April, May, and June) or the fall (October, November, and early December).

Here are some factors to consider in selecting the best time of year for your Ask Event:

- If you are already putting on a big fundraising event each year, in which month does it take place?
- If you are planning to convert or phase out that event, would it open up that time slot in your calendar for an Ask Event?
- If you were starting fresh, with no prior events to consider at all, when would be the ideal time to hold your Ask Event? What works best in the day-to-day life of your organization? Consider your existing annual calendar. For example, if your organization is a school, you might want to have the Ask Event in the spring, giving you the full prior school year to put on many well-attended Point of Entry Events.

Sample System of Events

Here is an example of one organization's completed System of Events chart.

CREATING YOUR SYSTEM OF EVENTS

Current Events	Convert Event to:			Ideal Month	Add/ Convert/ Eliminate by When
	Point of Entry Event Tour Stop	Point of Entry Conversion Event	Free Feel-Good Cultivation Event		
1. Golf outing					Eliminate now
2. Corporate-sponsored gala/auction		X		March	Convert year 1; eliminate year 2
3. Graduation			X	June	This year
4. Chess classes	X			Monthly	Now
5. Tutoring sessions	X			Monthly	Now
6. Holiday open house		X		December	This year
7. Volunteer recognition			X	April	This year
8. Speaking to Rotary club, realtors association				As requested	

Sample Event Calendars

To give you a sense of the careful consideration that goes into creating each organization's annual System of Events Calendar, here are two examples.

Nonprofit #1: Environmental Clean-Up Organization

- Two Point of Entry Events per month (including one Point of Entry in a Box per month)
- One Ask Event per year in the spring
- Two Free Feel-Good Cultivation Events per year:
  - One Free Feel-Good Cultivation Event for donors in your Multiple-Year Giving Society, held in August on a private boat
  - One Free Feel-Good Cultivation Event at year-end for all donors, held in conjunction with an awards picnic, celebrating volunteer clean-up crews
- Zero Point of Entry Conversion Events

Nonprofit #2: Domestic Violence Shelter

- Three Point of Entry Events per month (including one Point of Entry in a Box per month).
- One Ask Event per year in November
- Three Free Feel-Good Cultivation Events per year for donors:
  - The post-Ask Event Celebration in January, for everyone who made their Ask Event such a success.
  - A donor/volunteer recognition dinner or annual meeting with awards and a big-name speaker in the field of domestic violence, for all Multiple-Year Giving Society Donors.
  - A Sunday afternoon family picnic, called "Honoring Families" for donors and residents of the shelter.

But once you create your annual System of Events, inserting your mission into every event, the entire quality of your events will shift.

- One Point of Entry Conversion Event in March: corporate banquet—board chair's firm underwrites meal cost. Other corporations pay $10,000 to host tables; nets $100,000; 10-minute program while everyone is seated; Visionary Leader Talk, testimonial speaker; business cards given to table host if guests want more information.
- Two "third-party" events: outside groups organize the event, shelter's executive director gives Visionary Leader Talk, board member or alumni gives testimonial, executive director receives check for event proceeds.
  - Fashion show hosted by retailers who donate clothes to the shelter's new and gently-used clothing store.
  - Book-club event where local book clubs raise money for the shelter.

I hope these examples will help you go back and fill in your event conversion chart on page 234 and design the ideal System of Events for your organization.

Some words of encouragement: weeding out your most labor-intensive events will be the hardest part of this process. But once you create your annual System of Events, inserting your mission into every event, the entire quality of your events will shift. Rather than mopping up post-event paperwork and wondering what, if any, long-term impact your event will have, people will be *calling you* after the event to see how they can become involved. Rather than having staff members with limited time bogged down in planning the next event, your staff and volunteers will be ready and available to take those calls and stay with those donors through the cultivation process. In other words, it won't take many "missionized" events before the work of your existing staff can shift from putting on special events to applying themselves to major-gifts cultivation and asking, which are the key to sustainable funding.

For a much more detailed description of how to design a sustainable System of Events for your organization, including many real-life examples from our Benevon alumni groups, I encourage you to read my book, *Missionizing Your Special Events*.

CHAPTER 17

THE NEW NORMAL

If the Benevon message has taken hold in your thinking, a whole new view of individual fundraising will have opened up for you. The thought of asking strangers for money "cold" will forever trigger alarm bells and red flags. Putting on events that do not engage people in your work will become a thing of the past. Every event, meeting, or one-on-one conversation will become an opportunity for a Point of Entry or Point of Re-Entry Event. You will know that your job is to connect friends and donors to the passion and emotion of your work in addition to giving them the facts. You will recognize that you have no right to expect a true contribution from someone who has not been informed, inspired, listened to, and involved. You will trust your instincts about letting the donor determine the timing and pace of the relationship, ever vigilant of that donor's readiness to give again. You will know that the natural tendency of every person who has made a true contribution is to want to share that experience with others.

While this new view of fundraising might initially seem awkward and uncomfortable, eventually it will become second nature to you.

You don't have to overhaul everything at once.

Some groups start by focusing on one aspect of the Benevon Model. Which aspect do you think I would recommend? No doubt, the Point of Entry Event. If you are going to leave one lasting legacy from this model, make it

What if you became obsessed with doing impeccable follow-up after every contact with a donor or potential donor?

the one-hour Point of Entry, which will engage your community in your work and put an end to the "best-kept secret" syndrome. Commit to having at least two official Point of Entry Events per month. Then identify every other occasion where someone in your organization interfaces with the community. How could those individuals be engaged as Point of Entry guests or Ambassadors? How can you turn all of this into a system?

Other groups find they have no shortage of friends and donors. Their issue is getting to know their existing donors better as individuals. Those groups start with a Know-Thy-Donor program, getting re-acquainted with their donors and inviting them to special Points of Entry.

What if you became obsessed with doing impeccable follow-up after every contact with a donor or potential donor? What if each follow-up conversation was an opportunity to elicit their personal feedback with an eye to offering more of precisely what interested them? After six months to a year, even if you never held an Ask Event, that single focus would translate directly to your bottom line. That high-touch donor engagement naturally inspires donors to give, before you even ask them! After five years, you would have grown your base of long-term supporters exponentially.

Or perhaps you will choose to focus on asking. You may realize you have done more than enough in-depth cultivation and listening, yet no one has asked these loyal supporters to give in a big way. In that case, you are ready to establish your Multiple-Year Giving Society with Units of Service starting at $1,000 a year pledged for five years. Put together a Leadership or Challenge Gift and launch the program in earnest. This lets your loyal supporters know that now is the time to begin making their bigger gifts to you. You will finally be giving them the opportunity to contribute on a level commensurate with their passion about your work. Often they will wonder what has taken you so long to ask.

You will have established, one donor at a time, a base of lifelong supporters.

You may find that the only missing element of your program is giving your loyal donors a chance to introduce others. Your pool of donors, although large and generous, has stagnated over time. Your well-established, beloved organization is ready for an infusion of new energy. Beef up your Free Feel-Good Cultivation Events and encourage those cherished supporters to invite along a new friend or two. Encourage them to bring their families to a Point of Entry Event. Once there, tell them about the innovative new programs you are offering. Do the careful listening in the Follow-Up Call that will tell you how best to involve them. It will make the person who introduced them to you very happy.

This new potential donor may have come to the Point of Entry or Point of Re-Entry Event strictly to please their friend. But by the time they choose to give, they will feel so connected to your mission that their involvement with your organization will be a source of great personal fulfillment of their values and purpose. It will be their greatest privilege to make their gifts to your organization.

They will have raised their hands, and at least figuratively said, "Hey, look at me over here, you can count me in as part of the family. I want to be a part of the work you are doing. I really do understand what you're up to. Keep talking to me, keep teaching me more about the issues, keep involving me, and I will keep giving."

You will have established, one donor at a time, a base of lifelong supporters.

Your new fully-integrated process for engaging and developing meaningful relationships with lifelong individual donors will have become your "new normal." You will be well on the way to leaving a legacy of sustainable funding for your favorite nonprofit organization. And all of the hard work will have been worth it.

ABOUT THE AUTHOR

Terry Axelrod is the founder and CEO of Benevon, which has trained more than 4,000 nonprofit teams to implement the mission-based Benevon Model for Sustainable Funding over the past 16 years. This system engages and develops relationships with passionate and committed lifelong donors.

With nearly 40 years of experience in the nonprofit field, Axelrod has founded three nonprofit organizations in the fields of health care and affordable housing. She realized early in her career that the only path to sustainable funding was to systematically connect donors to the mission of the organization, then involve and cultivate them until they were clearly ready to give—in short, to treat donors the way you would treat a close friend or family member, someone with whom you planned to have a lifelong relationship.

She created the Benevon Model in 1996 after working at an inner-city Seattle school, where she designed and implemented the fundraising and marketing programs that yielded $7.2 million in two-and-a-half years.

Axelrod is an adjunct lecturer at the University of Michigan, where she received her Masters of Social Work and Bachelor of Arts degrees. She is a Life Trustee of Swedish Medical Center. She lives in Seattle, Washington with her husband, Alan.

ADDITIONAL INFORMATION AND RESOURCES

Visit our Web site at www.benevon.com to:

- Watch our free videos.
- Subscribe to our free electronic resources.
- Register for one of our many free introductory seminars or conference calls.
- Register for our Curriculum for Sustainable Funding.
- Purchase books and DVDs about Benevon.
- Learn about the Benevon Next Step donor-tracking system.

Other books by Terry Axelrod:

Raising More Money—
A Step-by-Step Guide to Building Lifelong Donors

Raising More Money—
The Point of Entry Handbook

Raising More Money—
The Ask Event Handbook

Beyond the Ask Event—
Fully Integrating the Benevon Model

The Joy of Fundraising

Missionizing Your Special Events

Videos by Terry Axelrod:

Introduction to Raising More Money

Re-Igniting Your Board

Seventeen Minutes to Sustainable Funding

Creating Sustainable Funding for Your Nonprofit

INDEX